This is the first appearance in English of a brilliant, exciting and controversial book which has enjoyed tremendous success since its first appearance in Germany in 1971. Translated from the German by Arnold Pomerans, *The Making of Human Aggression* was written by Herbert Selg, Wilfried Belschner, Ute Jakobi, Gottfried Lischke and Franz Schott, under the general editorship of Herbert Selg.

Herbert Selg studied psychology and spent several years in educational advisory posts. He then lectured at the Universities of Göttingen and Freiburg, and since 1968 has been Professor of Psychology at the Niedersachen Training College, Brunswick.

Bob Green is Foundation Professor of Psychology at the Open University. In his foreword to this book he points out that our child-rearing habits and educational systems will eventually have to take into account what we already know about the nature of aggression. Whether we like it or not a moral choice is involved, and the sooner we face up to where our values lie the better our chances of avoiding the final consequences of untrammelled violence as expressed in war and social disorder.

# THE MAKING OF
# HUMAN AGGRESSION

## A Psychological Approach

Edited by HERBERT SELG

With a Foreword by
BOB GREEN

ST. MARTIN'S PRESS, NEW YORK

Library of Congress Cataloging in Publication Data

Selg, Herbert, 19

    The making of human aggres

    Translatio      Zur Aggression verda
    "Translated from the German by Arnold Pomerans."
    Bibliography: p.
    1. Aggressiveness (Psychology)   I. Title.
[DNLM: 1. Aggression.   2. Psychology.   BF575.A3 M235]
BF575.A3S4313   1975b   155.2'4   75-9499

FOREWORD by Bob Green  1

EDITOR'S PREFACE  5

1  *The Frustration-Aggression Hypothesis*  9
   Herbert Selg

2  *The Aggressive Instinct*  41
   Ute Jakobi, Herbert Selg and Wilfried Belschner

3  *Learning and Aggression*  61
   Wilfried Belschner

4  *The Psychobiology of Aggression*  107
   Gottfried Lischke

5  *What is Aggression?*  141
   Franz Schott

EDITOR'S POSTSCRIPT  173

POSTSCRIPT TO THE SECOND
   (GERMAN) EDITION  179

BIBLIOGRAPHY  181

*Professor Robert T. Green*

# FOREWORD

Current interest in aggression as a subject ripe for scientific enquiry can be traced back into the last century. Yet only in the past decade or so has man's inhumanity to man gripped the imagination of the general public in the sense of being hailed as a socially significant topic. Largely in response to theories that said more for their proponents' creative gifts than for their concern with the empirical data, people innocent of the techniques of contemporary behavioural science began to look to sociology, social anthropology, ethology, and what might be charitably termed the animal behaviour soap operas, for answers to the problems associated with human aggression.

Ethologists in the days of Darwin and the Fabres, by the way, were better known as naturalists – a label that possibly reflected their painstaking ability to make accurate observations of natural phenomena in an unpretentious manner.

Instinct theories, by Tinbergen and Lorenz out of Freud, offered descriptive accounts that explained everything and predicted nothing. Still less did they pave the way to cure or

1

control. In consequence, they were highly attractive in certain quarters. By analysing the problem they either managed to explain it away or left mankind awaiting its doom, the helpless victim of primeval forces that relieved him of all responsibility for his atrocities, whether on a domestic, international or cosmic scale.

While it would take a rash man to suggest that modern psychology has finally resolved all our difficulties in this area, it would be equally perverse to ignore what has been achieved. To put it modestly, we have arrived at a better understanding of the part played by learning in the development of aggressive behaviour. More particularly, we are beginning to appreciate the profound influence exerted by our child-rearing practices. Violence, especially of the ritualized variety, when indulged in by a parent or teacher, has some peculiar effects – not all of which would be thought socially desirable by a disinterested observer from another planet. Recent work indicates that beating a child is more readily understood as an expression of malice, rather than being the serious educational endeavour we are invited to believe on behalf of those adults who have trouble socializing their own aggressive impulses.

So the way ahead, although by no means clear, is hopefully acquiring some signposts. Of one thing we may be certain; our child-rearing habits and educational systems fifty years from now will no longer rest on folklore and inspired – more often uninspired – guesswork. We are beginning to see how it is that man, that most civilized of creatures, can derive satisfaction from destroying his fellows and himself. With that knowledge we can hope to present the world to him in a light that will offer him greater satisfaction from pursuing more constructive enterprises.

The main message of this book, then, is one of hope rather than despair. Behaviour is modifiable, human behaviour more so than that of any other animal. All around us we see acts of aggression; but also we see acts of kindness and cooperation, of love as well as hate, of compassion as well as cruelty. Since man, by his nature, is not irrevocably locked into any one form of behaviour, it is for him to choose what he will be. He is at least as capable of choosing the better as he is of choosing the worse. But choose he must. That *is* part of his nature. Other animals must suffer what the Fates decree. Only man can make a moral choice. To abdicate that choice is to abandon mankind.

BOB GREEN
*22 July 1974*

# EDITOR'S PREFACE

Those who pick up this book may wonder with some irritation if there is any need for yet another work on aggression, when so many have appeared during the past few years. The answer is that most of these books, and particularly those published in Germany, are not lacking in bias. It is for this reason that our five authors have tried to give a necessarily brief account of all the most important theories about human aggression. Their contributions will make it clear, quite incidentally, that serious research into aggression is also the best way of studying the conditions of world peace.

Chapter 1 deals with the frustration-aggression hypothesis, now thirty years old but recently revived. Chapter 2 looks at instinctive models of aggression which have become very fashionable, but which, as this entire book tries to demonstrate, are scientifically unsubstantiated and socially harmful. All talk of an aggressive instinct is dangerous; it helps to foster aggressive attitudes and increases the danger of war.

In Chapter 3, Dr Belschner discusses what would appear to be the most useful theory of the origins of human aggression: man adopts aggressive attitudes chiefly by learning through success and imitation.

In Chapter 4, Dr Lischke deals with the psychophysiology of aggression and shows convincingly how little substance there is to the popular view that the brain contains aggressive centres or that special aggressive substances have been isolated in the blood.

In Chapter 5, Franz Schott offers a fundamental critique of all research into aggression, and calls for far more reflective studies.

Finally, in the Postscript, the main arguments of this book are summarized for the reader's convenience.

The layout of the book is such that we felt free to dispense with an index. The bibliography, by contrast, is comprehensive, so that the critical reader may, if he so wishes, check every assertion by consulting the sources.

It is impossible to mention by name all those to whom we are indirectly indebted. We hope that this omission will not be thought ungrateful or arrogant.

HERBERT SELG
*Brunswick, Summer 1971*

*Herbert Selg*

# 1. THE FRUSTRATION-AGGRESSION HYPOTHESIS

# 1. THE FRUSTRATION-AGGRESSION HYPOTHESIS

## 1. The frustration-aggression hypothesis

Whereas instinct theory (see Chapter 2) tends to treat aggression as a spontaneous phenomenon, the frustration-aggression (F-A) hypothesis considers aggression to be a purely reactive form of behaviour. It is with this hypothesis, framed by Dollard, Doob, Miller, Mowrer and Sears in 1939, that the present chapter will be chiefly concerned.

Few psychological theories are more highly organized or have more easily verified consequences than the frustration-aggression hypothesis. This largely explains its invigorating effect on psychological research.

## THE GENERAL ASSUMPTIONS OF THE FRUSTRATION-AGGRESSION HYPOTHESIS

### The basic assumptions

The central theorem of the F-A hypothesis states that 'aggression is always a consequence of frustration' and, conversely, that 'the existence of frustration always leads to

9

some form of aggression'. These interrelated hypotheses contain two concepts requiring definition: namely frustration and aggression.

*Frustration* is the blocking of an organism's path towards a goal. Thus if a small boy sets out to buy an ice-cream, and if all the ice-cream has been sold, the boy suffers frustration (Dollard *et al.*). Although Dollard *et al.* do not say so expressly,[1] their definition is usually taken to refer to the blocking stimulus (the ice-cream is sold out) and not to the associated subjective experience (the boy's disappointment or irritation).

*Aggression* is any series of actions whose goal response is injury to another organism or its substitute. According to Dollard, when the small boy fails to obtain his ice-cream, he may yell, stamp his feet or curse the vendor. In other words, he inflicts the 'injury' in a purely symbolic way.

*Supplementary assumptions*

The F-A hypothesis also makes the following, subsidiary, assumptions:

1. The intensity of the aggressive response depends on the intensity of the frustration, i.e. it is determined by
   – the intensity of the blocked activity (the sudden withdrawal of food leads to greater aggression in a very hungry child than it does in one who has just been fed).
   – the intensity of the block (the postponement of a holiday by one hour produces less aggression than a longer delay),
   – and the number of blocks (we generally suffer one minor block without showing aggression, but may lose our temper after a whole series of such blocks).
2. If aggression is likely to be punished, it may become *inhibited*. The more probable the punishment, the more unlikely the aggression.
3. Aggression due to frustration is directed most strongly against the frustrator.

10

If the tendency to attack the frustrator is strongly blocked, the aggression may become *displaced*: the attack is redirected against another object, or the frustrator may be attacked obliquely (instead of assassinating a hateful politician, we merely tell jokes at his expense).

4. If the aggression against the frustrator or against possible substitutes is very strongly blocked, the result may be self-aggression, a special type of displacement. This happens particularly when we are forced to think of ourselves as the source of our own frustration (for instance when we fail an examination after inadequate preparation).

5. The active expression of aggression diminishes the tendency to aggress (the so-called catharsis hypothesis).

## THE ORIGINS OF THE F-A HYPOTHESIS

Important elements of the F-A hypothesis are derived from older theories. Dollard *et al.* trace its history back to Karl Marx, who argued in the *Communist Manifesto* (1848) that the exploitation of the workers so frustrates them that they are bound, sooner or later, to rise up against their oppressors.

Freud, too, came close to the F-A hypothesis when he explained during the First World War that aggression results from the non-satisfaction of sexual impulses. From 1920 onwards, however, he treated aggression as a derivative of the so-called death instinct.

It was from Freud that Dollard *et al.* borrowed the concept of 'displacement', and turned it into the cornerstone of their supplementary assumptions. Although the elements of the F-A hypothesis were not new, it was only in Dollard's[2] relatively concise and trenchant formulation that the theory was opened up to empirical verification and refutation. Dollard *et al.* produced few systematic observations of their own, and preferred to appeal to 'common sense'.

In fact, by 1939, Dollard *et al.* had come to look upon their

11

second basic assumption – namely that the existence of frustration always leads to some form of aggression – as a purely heuristic principle, i.e. as an educational method challenging the pupil to discover laws and principles for himself. Dollard *et al.* also mentioned other effects of frustration, for instance, substitute actions and rational solutions, but they did not enter into details.

In 1941, N. E. Miller amended the second basic assumption of the F-A hypothesis to read: 'Frustration produces instigations to a number of different types of response, one of which is an instigation to aggression.' However, both he and R. R. Sears (1941) retained the first basic assumption, i.e. that aggression is always a consequence of frustration.

## 2. The subsequent history of the frustration-aggression hypothesis

In due course, the F-A hypothesis came to share the fate of every new scientific theory: it was examined critically and modified. Here and there, however, it suffered so much conceptual distortion that 'frustration' came to mean nearly all things to all men.

Unlike Rosenzweig (1934), who had originally treated all defects, losses and conflicts as frustrations, Dollard *et al.*, as we saw, considered frustration to be contingent upon the blocking of an organism's path to a goal. Most students using the empirical approach have tried to keep to this definition, though, like Buss (1961) and Berkowitz (1962), they do not always interpret it in the same way. The definition mentioned in the preceding section leaves the types of (external) stimulus that may be called 'frustrations' an open question.

Other writers use 'frustration' to refer to the emotional and motivational ('inner') effects of disturbing stimuli. Brown and Farber (1951), for instance, treat frustration as an 'intervening variable' or as a 'hypothetical construct' (i.e. a derived and not a directly observable magnitude). Others again use the term 'frustration' in both senses (Bandura and Walters 1964).

We think it much better to introduce a clear, conceptual distinction between the disturbing (external) stimulus and its emotional (internal) sequelae. Thus we shall reserve the term 'frustration' for the stimulus, and call the inner effects 'frustration states' or 'frustration-experiences'.

## CLASSIFICATION OF FRUSTRATIONS

It is mainly thanks to the empirical studies of Buss (1961) that the thesis of Dollard *et al.* has been clarified and systematized. According to Buss, angry responses are only one of many observable forms of aggression, not all of which can necessarily be traced back to frustration. In addition to aggression-releasing stimuli, Buss also admits the class of noxious stimuli (including physical attacks) and annoyers (e.g. the smell of garlic on another's breath):

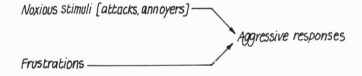

Buss rightly objects to the lumping of both together under the general heading of 'frustrations'. A scene described as frustration by Doob and Sears (1939) – a drunk spilling some food, whisky or cigarette ash over someone at a party – must, according to Buss, be classified as an annoyer, since it did not involve the blocking of ongoing behaviour. Spilling ash at a party only constitutes a frustration if it interferes with, say, the intention to take a partner on to the dance floor.

Buss also refuses to treat as valid contributions to the F-A hypothesis experiments in which the experimenter annoys the subject 'out of the blue'. In many experiments, moreover, verbal attacks are treated as 'frustrations', but we are entitled to wonder whether such attacks have the same goal-blocking effects on all subjects, and whether it is not far better to treat them as noxious stimuli.

Since – despite Buss's objection – experiments in which the subjects are annoyed rather than blocked are often described as F-A studies, we must make a clear distinction between frustration in both the strict and the broad sense:

A *frustration in the strict sense* is the blocking of a goal-directed activity; a *frustration in the broad sense* may be any unpleasant experience whatsoever, not least a lack of instinctual satisfaction. Only when used in the strict sense does 'frustration' constitute a useful scientific term; when used in the broad sense it can be applied to so wide a range of phenomena as to become quite meaningless.

We shall not be looking at the many experimental attempts to subsume frustrations under broader categories – by, for instance, considering them special cases of denied or delayed rewards or negative reinforcements, e.g. punishments (cf. Amsel 1958; Lawrence and Festinger 1962; Bandura and Walters 1964). Nor shall we be discussing the many experiments designed to elucidate the role of pain as an elicitor of aggression (cf. Scott 1958; Rachman 1965; Azrin *et al.* 1965, 1968; Kahn and Kirk 1968, Ulrich 1969). These omissions should not be mistaken for critical judgements.

FRUSTRATION AND ITS EFFECTS

*Behavioural results*

*Non-aggressive behaviour following frustration:* There are two frustration theories that differ from F-A theory but which are no less one-sided. According to the *frustration-regression hypothesis* advanced by Barker, Dembo and Lewin (1941), frustration is followed by a type of behaviour that can be equated with regression (in Freud's sense). Thus, during experiments, frustrated children often evince 'primitive' forms of behaviour reminiscent of earlier phases of mental development. An adult who pummels his radio with his fists whenever reception is poor would show similar regressive behaviour.

The *frustration-fixation hypothesis* of Maier (1949) is based on the following experiment: a rat, having learned to distinguish between two cards with different markings, is forced to leap through the air. If it jumps at Card 1, it is admitted to some food; if it jumps at Card 2, it drops into the net beneath (Figure 1).

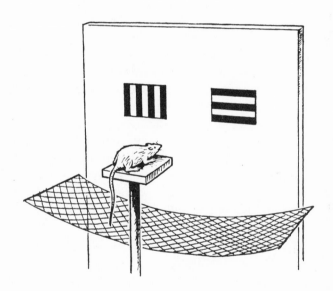

Fig 1 Maiers experimental set-up (after Lashley)

The position of the cards is changed, and when the rat has learned to jump only at the card giving it access to the food, the experimenter presents it with a totally insoluble problem: the rat is rewarded or punished quite arbitrarily for jumping at either of the two cards. The rat reacts to this change in a stereotyped way: it ignores the markings and jumps in one direction only, for instance to the right. This type of reaction becomes so rigid in some of the rats that, even when they are shown the food beside one of the cards, they continue to jump in the direction they had originally chosen. Their behaviour is reminiscent of a man 'knocking his head against a wall'.

In more recent books, the effects of frustration have been described less one-sidedly; in particular, their authors list a large number of non-aggressive reactions that might follow upon frustration. Bandura and Walters (1964) mention dependency behaviour, withdrawal, apathy, somatization, autistic thinking, regression and constructive mastery of the situation. It should be noted that all but the last of these reactions have a negative connotation.

The constructive solution merits closer investigation, the more so as all forms of education aim at increasing the probability of constructive behaviour. One of the best-known experiments in this field has been published by Davitz (1952), who showed that the way in which seven- to nine-year-olds respond to frustration depends on their training. Thus children who have been rewarded consistently for aggressive-competitive behaviour will react to experimental frustration in predominantly aggressive ways, while children who have been rewarded for constructive-cooperative behaviour will react in more constructive ways.

Further evidence that *learning* plays an important role in this sphere has been adduced by Chittenden (1942), who, with the help of films depicting positive responses to frustration, was able to reduce the aggressive reactions of highly aggressive children. Other observations suggest just as clearly that it is possible to teach non-aggressive behaviour to frustrated subjects (cf. Bateson 1941; Bandura 1962; Taylor and Epstein 1967).

From what we have said, it would follow that the *two basic assumptions of F-A theory* – that (a) aggression is always a consequence of frustration, and (b) the existence of frustration always leads to some form of aggression – *are untenable.*

*Aggressive behaviour after frustration:* For all that, many psychologists continue to maintain that aggression is the most tangible consequence of frustration. On what evidence or assumption do they base this view?

On the simplest assumption – left open by Dollard *et al.* – aggression is an innate response to frustration. However, once it is granted that many forms of behaviour following frustration cannot be called aggression, then even this thesis must fall by the wayside.

Aggressive acts are generally intensive forms of behaviour (see particularly Bandura and Walters (1964)). Thus the low-intensity, slow and relatively relaxed application of the mother's hand to the child's head is called 'stroking', but its intensive application is called a 'slap'.

Especially during the first years of life, when we adopt our basic behaviour patterns, the acquisition of aggressive responses (with or without frustration) must prove highly advantageous. An infant trying to pull a resistant object into his cot, may start to jerk at it, i.e. use force. This will often prove successful, and thus pave the way for the kind of intensive behaviour that far too often strikes us as aggression. The child might, however, fail to solve the problem by force, in which case he might stop jerking and start screaming instead. For this reaction, too, he may receive a quick reward – parents do not react as speedily to softer noises: only when their peace of mind is shattered do they rush up to the child, thus reinforcing his noisy behaviour. In dealing with his siblings, and with other children as well, a child quickly learns to appreciate the advantages of the type of goal-directed behaviour usually termed 'aggressive'. Thus, when trying to get hold of a toy, he may well discover that snatching is far more effective than kindness.

In this sphere, as in so many others, learning from a model

17

(through observation or imitation, see Chapter 3) plays a most important role.

Children often watch an older child getting his way by being aggressive towards a younger one. Adults applying corporal punishment provide them with a further 'example' of highly aggressive behaviour, and television daily demonstrates how simple it is to get one's way by knocking one's opponent down. Children take television films very seriously, and murderous aggression must strike them as one of the most obvious features of adult 'interhuman' behaviour.[3]

Indeed, even playful contacts between parents and children often help to reinforce aggressive behaviour. Thus, when a ten- to twelve-month-old child 'smacks' his father, his action is often reinforced by the hilarity of adults who consider it 'sweet' or 'funny'.

In short, aggressive behaviour is easily learned because it is so often crowned with success. Only parents following a deliberate educational plan do not foster aggression in their children. Whenever parents pay heed to a screaming or stamping child, be it to silence or to punish him, they are, in fact, reinforcing his rebelliousness by their very attention. (The only neutral, non-reinforcing parental reaction is to ignore the rebellious child unostentatiously.)

*Constructive* methods of coping with frustration are much more difficult to learn. Whenever we react aggressively, we do not have to evaluate a complex situation or to choose among motor responses. To cope with frustration *constructively*, by contrast, we must have a grasp of the overall situation and apply a particular motor pattern.

Take the following example: a child wants to run into the garden, but is frustrated because the back door is locked with the key on the child's side. At the age of only fifteen months he may respond by tugging at the key, kicking at the door or screaming until someone comes to his aid. The child cannot yet apply the constructive solution, i.e. to turn the key; this he will not learn until he is three, four or even five years old.

Seen in this light, it is no wonder that we learn from our *early successes*, and from the example of others, that *it pays to react to frustration with aggression*, and particularly that aggression is a useful instrument for escaping from frustrating situations. Buss (1963, 1966) has demonstrated experimentally that frustration often leads to instrumental aggression.

## The emotional effects of frustration

*The anger/rage effect:* The adoption of aggressive reactions to frustrations may well be encouraged by the anger or rage effect.

Berkowitz (1962), who has, incidentally, acknowledged his debt to the Yale group (Dollard *et al.*), stresses the importance of emotional reactions to frustration, which he identifies with rage and anger, and which, he claims, the old F-A hypothesis tends to neglect. He believes that this emotional reaction may be innate[4] and that aggression, in its turn, may be an innate response to rage and anger. However, he believes that this cycle may be broken by learning.

But much as the old F-A theory was imperfect because frustration does not inevitably lead to aggression, so Berkowitz's reformulation, too, is vitiated by the fact that frustration is not invariably followed by rage or anger – his position becomes untenable as soon as we ask how the anger/rage reaction can be demonstrated. Experiments into emotional responses (cf. Schachter and Singer 1962; Schachter and Wheeler 1962) have produced the startling conclusion that human beings stimulated by artificial means tend to associate their experiences with sensations the experimenter has just described to them.

Thus subjects injected with adrenaline and told about its physiological effects (e.g. palpitations) do not allow themselves to be provoked by aggressive models.[5] Others, by contrast, who have been misinformed or not informed about

19

the effects of adrenaline, react in aggressive or silly ways, depending on the behaviour of the model, and describe their emotions accordingly.

The response to one and the same state of physiological excitation may therefore be described as rage, pleasure or indifference, depending on situational suggestions (see Chapter 4). This might indicate that though frustrations, like reflexes, cause a measurable degree of excitation, the latter need not necessarily go hand in hand with rage and anger. True, if from childhood we are misled into thinking that human beings react to frustration with rage, this effect is bound to be handed down from one generation to the next.

*The frustration-drive hypothesis:* As we have suggested, the frustration-aggression hypothesis reduces, via the frustration-anger/rage hypothesis, to a non-specific frustration-drive or frustration-excitation hypothesis. By excitation we refer here to a measurable change in the frustrated person, regardless of the experimental content. This hypothesis was first advanced by Amsel (1951) and Brown (1961), and developed by Bandura and Walters (1964).

The frustration-drive hypothesis, unlike its predecessors, is no longer an aggression-specific assumption.[6] It covers more than the purely aggressive reactions to frustration: it explains why, after frustration, all reactions become intensive. An experiment, occasionally adduced in support of the old F-A hypothesis, but, in fact, interpreted much better in terms of the frustration-drive hypothesis, was made by Haner and Brown (1955). They measured the pressure exerted by children on a plunger as a dependent frustration variable: after frustration, the pressure increased significantly. Quite obviously this experiment does not probe into aggression as such and therefore falls in the province of the frustration-drive hypothesis rather than the F-A hypothesis. Further proof of the usefulness of the frustration-drive hypothesis may be found in Bandura and Walters (1964); Silverman and Kleinman (1967); and Geen and O'Neal (1969).

To test a thesis advanced by Selg, Draht has investigated the effect of frustration on 'hand-test'[7] variables.

Two groups of primary schoolchildren (Grades 3 and 4), classified by their classmates as aggressive or non-aggressive respectively, were divided into experimental and control groups. The experimental groups were frustrated: they were asked to take a preliminary dictation, and each one was told separately immediately prior to the 'hand test' proper that he had done badly, and that, in general, his recent school work was poor. Since it was uncertain whether this mis-information caused frustration in the strict sense (e.g. whether the children were disappointed by the results of the dictation) they were also told, again before the beginning of the 'hand test', that they would be given a piece of chocolate if they could tell the price of the slab lying on the table. Whatever price they happened to mention was said to be the correct one, but, they were told: 'You can't have the choco-late, all the same, because the question was much too easy.'

|  | Aggressive | Non-aggressive | Total |
|---|---|---|---|
| Frustrated (experimental group) | 15 | 13 | 28 |
| Non-frustrated (control group) | 13 | 12 | 25 |
| Total | 28 | 25 | 53 |

Next came the 'hand test' proper, after which the children were told that their dictation had never been assessed and that their teachers would, in any case, not be informed.

The experimental and the control groups both produced the same average AOS (acting-out score). In other words, frustration had not led to an increase in aggressive tendencies, as the F-A theory claims it should have done (and as, inci-

21

dentally, the author himself believed it would). However, it did appear that the frustrated children had a much more highly dispersed AOS than the rest. This meant that though frustration had indeed led to an increase of the aggressive tendencies of various children, in others it had led to an increase in the 'antipodes' of aggression (aff + dep + com + fear).[8] Thus the children with the six highest AO scores (in whom the aggressive tendency had been increased by frustration) as well as those with the four lowest AO scores (in whom there had been an increase in the other tendencies) came from the frustrated group. This result must be considered evidence in favour of the frustration-drive hypothesis and against the F-A hypothesis.

Let us sum up: even if we adopt the frustration-drive hypothesis, we must grant that the anger/rage effect is a common, and aggression the most probable, behavioural consequence of frustration. Frustration intensifies the drive, and makes it likely that every subsequent reaction will be of high intensity. (As we mentioned earlier, on page 17, intensive behaviour is readily classified as aggression.)

In support of this assumption we should also like to mention an experiment by Walters and Brown (1964): children whose high-intensity behaviour had been reinforced were far more frequently classified as 'aggressive' than children whose low-intensity behaviour had been reinforced.

### Situational influences

*Situational interpretation as an intervening variable:* In experimental studies of frustration it is essential to establish whether what is being investigated is, in fact, frustration in the strict sense. In other words, it has to be shown that ongoing goal-directed activities have been blocked. To that end, the experimental subject must be questioned very thoroughly and the experimenter cannot leave it at mere observations of overt behaviour (behaviourism).

Pastore (1952) has given an impressive experimental

demonstration of the importance of subjective situational interpretations in frustration experiments. In particular, he has shown that arbitrary frustrations are more likely to cause aggression than 'reasonable' frustrations do. However, although it is understandable that the latter should elicit weaker reactions than the former, the results obtained so far cannot be fitted into a single theory. [9]

It would also seem that the status of the frustrator has some bearing on the effects of frustration (Hokanson and Shetler 1961). Aggression is less pronounced against persons of high status than it is against persons of low status (cf. Thibaut and Riecken 1955; Berkowitz 1962).

Finally, a frustrated person becomes more excited when he is blocked while in sight of his goal than he does when he is frustrated at the beginning of his activity (Haner and Brown 1955).

*The importance of cues:* Whether frustration leads to aggression, even when aggression has been learned as the chief reaction to frustration, depends on further situational characteristics as well. Bindra (1959) and Berkowitz (1962) have stressed the importance of cues: a stimulus, even if experienced as anger or rage, leads to aggression only in the presence of a suitable object, i.e. an object that elicits aggression by means of special cues. The most suitable object is, no doubt, the frustrator, if one is available. According to Berkowitz, objects resembling the frustrator can also trigger off aggression (on displacement, see pages 26-8 below). However, when he writes (1962, p. 33) that these objects need merely be present in the thwarted person's imagination, he considerably weakens his argument, for such objects cannot be investigated empirically – it is only too easy to discover 'symbolic' cues for every act of aggression.

Perhaps the most convincing argument in favour of cues was provided by Holst and von St Paul (1962):

When a cock was stimulated by scalp electrodes in the

appropriate areas, he attacked all sort of objects, e.g. stuffed birds of prey, the experimenter's hand, etc.; but, in the absence of a suitable 'substitute enemy', he merely showed motor agitation. Similarly, cats stimulated by scalp electrodes showed no 'free-wheeling' aggression (Roberts and Kiess 1964): 89 per cent attacked a cloth dog, 33 per cent a rubber rat, but not a single one attacked a lump of wood.

Human experiments in support of his assumption have been conducted by Berkowitz and Rawlings (1963), Geen (1966) and Knurek (1969). For a critical summary, see Baron and Kepner (1970).

The validity of the first supplementary assumption of F-A theory (see page 10) – i.e. that the intensity of the aggressive response depends on the intensity of the frustration – was questioned long ago (see, for instance, Buss 1961). It is weakened further by the existence of the situational variables we have just described.

## THE INHIBITION OF AGGRESSION

One of the most important additional hypotheses of F-A theory concerns the inhibition, or blocking, of aggression (see page 11). Inhibition is not the same as the absence of aggression. Where there is no tendency to display aggression, there is also no need to inhibit it, but where aggressive tendencies are present, aggression can be avoided by inhibition.

Punishments are constantly used to produce inhibitions, though punishments are not really suited to this end. Learning theory has shown that punishment of a lapse will only militate against its repetition if such punishment is meted out there and then. This means that a thief would have to be caught and punished at the scene of his crime.

Corporal punishment of children, too, is futile. Parents resorting to corporal punishment often have exceptionally aggressive children (see Glueck and Glueck 1950; Sears *et al.* 1953; Bandura and Walters 1963). This may well be due to the fact that, with such punishment, the parents supply the children with aggressive models (Eron *et al.* 1963). A calm discussion of what is permissible and what is not is much more effective with children than corporal punishment.

Experiments with 'aggression machines' in which subjects do not see their victims often have an aggression-reducing effect on non-sadistic and non-frustrated subjects (Milgram 1966). A similar reduction usually ensues when male subjects are told that their 'victim' is of the opposite sex (the 'chivalry effect'; cf. Buss 1961; Selg 1968).

The correct social strategy for reducing aggressiveness and improving the chances of world peace must therefore be based on keeping the learning of aggressive responses down to a bare minimum rather than on the construction of the appropriate inhibitions. Inhibitions have proved exceedingly fragile; moreover, when we teach children to inhibit their aggressiveness we often find that we have inhibited their more positive responses as well.

Thus when a father beats his child for aggressive behaviour, he does not so much inhibit aggression as make the child feel generally ill at ease in his presence.

Special tests (Selg 1968) suggest that criminals, far from being 'uninhibited', as one might have expected them to be, either merely lack strong enough inhibitive mechanisms to offset their aggressive tendencies or else are unable to apply their general inhibitions to relatively unfamiliar situations. Thus they may have learned not to beat up their parents whenever the latter annoy them, but they are unable to extend this inhibition to their contacts with irritating strangers.

The F-A definition of inhibition must therefore be reframed as follows: if an aggressive act is likely to be punished (or to fail), the act may be inhibited – the greater the expectation of punishment, the more likely the inhibition. However, high expectations that aggression will be punished usually go

25

hand in hand with a general expectation of punishment and failure. Such expectations may therefore be part of a general (neurotic) disturbance.

## DISPLACEMENT

The third supplementary assumption of the F-A hypo-thesis (see page 11) states that aggression may be shifted from the frustrator to a more or less neutral object, or change its form.

According to Berkowitz, the displacement of aggression from one object to another can only take place if the two emit similar stimuli, although, as we have noted, it is extremely difficult to isolate such stimuli or to refute their existence. In other words, advocates of the displacement hypothesis must first of all define the term 'similarity'. So far, all we have been offered are circular arguments: an object is attacked because of its resemblance to the original target, and its resemblance to the latter is inferred from its being attacked.

Far better, therefore, to reinterpret 'displacement' with the help of the more recent frustration-anger/rage or of the frustration-drive hypothesis. Today we know that a strong affect, or an exaggerated drive, has an unfavourable effect on task performance (the Yerkes-Dodson Law; see Figure 2). Thus, while slight examination anxiety increases the desire to

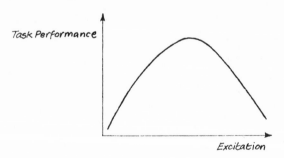

Fig 2  The Yerkes-Dodson Law

26

work, strong fear reduces the powers of concentration and hence the quality of the preparatory study.

Aggression usually reflects a state of high arousal, so high, in fact, that it generally interferes with mental work (see Latané and Arrowood 1963); in the present context this means that it reduces the ability to distinguish between stimuli. Thus a woman who can normally tell Dick from Harry may, when excited, say that 'Men are all the same', and vent her fury on Harry if she cannot lay her hands on Dick.

It is more helpful to speak of 'generalization' and 'discrimination', terms that apply to all forms of behaviour, than to postulate an aggression- or conflict-specific form of 'displacement': it is because they have learned to discriminate that children may be cheeky at home and well-behaved at school, or vice versa; it is for lack of discrimination that people get into a 'blind rage' once they have been 'pushed beyond the limit'.

The term 'displacement' should only be used when it is quite obvious that an aggressive act is, despite the subject's ability to discriminate, directed, not at the original object but at a neutral one. Thus we might speak of displacement when a boy, having been frustrated by his father, beats up another child in the street without apparent cause. However, when – and this is the usual criterion of displacement – all that can be proved is that boys who are frequently beaten by their parents are more aggressive outside than inside the home, then this points less to displacement than to successful discrimination: such children have learned not to take insults in the street lying down, and that aggression is more successfully directed against peers than against parents.

This is perhaps the place to say a few words about the 'scapegoat hypothesis' often mentioned in the context of displacement. Special cases in point are the Jews, who, in fact, first introduced the term. Jews have been persecuted repeatedly and over centuries – poor crops or any other mis-

THE MAKING OF HUMAN AGGRESSION

fortunes were invariably blamed on them. But is this reaction really explained by the hypothesis? It leaves far too many questions unanswered. Why were the Jews such favourite scapegoats? We can do no more than speculate about the beginnings of antisemitism, recalling the fact, for instance, that Christians used to consider all Jews as deicides, or hated them for the fact that, though they were witnesses to the life of the historical Jesus, they refused to believe in him and hence forced a measure of unbearable uncertainty ('cognitive dissonance') upon the Christians themselves.

If we ask how individuals acquire antisemitic prejudices, the most probable answer is by imitation. Thus it is simply because modern German children have never witnessed antisemitic excesses that German antisemitism has become a spent force. Yet another form of 'displacement' can be traced back to the same learning mechanism that governs so many other forms of human behaviour.

The *function* of a particular scapegoat depends on the historical circumstances. Sometimes the persecution of scapegoats is rooted in childhood resentment; at other times it is due to governmental incompetence; last but not least it may be a response to apparently inexplicable events (e.g. the Plague in the Middle Ages). One thing is certain, however: a society that treats a minority as a scapegoat does not reduce its overall aggressive tendencies but creates further aggression (as witness the origins of the Second World War).


### SELF-DIRECTED AGGRESSION

According to the F-A hypothesis, self-directed aggression only appears when the aggressive response to frustration cannot be turned against the frustrator or a similar object, or when there is reason to seek the cause of the frustration in one's own inadequacies.

It is one of the simplest assumptions of writers on aggression that every man possesses a fixed quantum of aggression or aggressiveness. If part of the available aggressiveness can be directed against others, less is apparently left over for self-directed aggression, and vice versa.[10] But this theory is mere armchair psychology.

Those who have realized that human behaviour is largely a matter of learning[11] will also appreciate that self-directed, no less than other-directed aggression, can be learned more or less independently: children readily imitate the overt behaviour of adults. Thus if a child becomes the object of repeated acts of aggression, e.g. of constant nagging, he may adopt the same attitude and become permanently dissatisfied with himself.

In this connection, we ought really to speak of 'aggressions' and 'types of aggressiveness' rather than of 'aggression' or 'aggressiveness'. Thus while the aggressiveness of some is predominantly verbal, that of others is mainly physical. Some may combine both types; others, again, may display neither. Again, some may direct their aggression chiefly against weaker subjects, while others direct it against strangers, against themselves, against others as well as against themselves, etc. It is pointless to attach the same amount of aggressiveness to the philosophical debate between Father Copleston, s.j., and Bertrand Russell (Russell 1957) as to a fight between two drunks.

One questionnaire (Selg 1968) suggests that self- and other-directed aggression, far from being inversely proportional, are in direct ratio – the 'self-directed aggression' scale was found to have the following correlation[12] with the sum of 'other-directed aggression' scales:

| | | |
|---|---|---|
| 1. | Female students | $+ \cdot 498$ |
| 2. | Male students | $+ \cdot 457$ |
| 3. | Soldiers | $+ \cdot 435$ |
| 4. | Criminals | $+ \cdot 333$ |

The self-aggression score of criminals, no less than their other-directed aggression score, was well above the average.

29

## CATHARSIS

The view of Dollard *et al.* that self-directed is inter-changeable with other-directed aggression leads us straight to the last supplementary assumption of F-A theory, namely catharsis. According to that assumption, the active expression of aggression diminishes the tendency to aggress.

The catharsis hypothesis is a development of ideas first propounded by Aristotle, who contended that catharsis, or the purging of the emotions, could be achieved by such vicarious experiences as the drama. This theory has adherents to this day. The film and television industries never tire of defending vicious films by reference to their alleged cathartic effects.

Aristotle's theory, however, is refuted by an impressive body of systematic observations. Here we shall merely mention a study by Bandura, Ross and Ross (1963) in-volving ninety-six three- to six-year-old children.

The children were divided into three experimental groups and one control group. All three experimental groups were shown various aggressive acts with which they were unlikely to be familiar (for instance, smashing the head of a large doll with a hammer). These acts were demonstrated to the first group by live adult models, to the second group by adults on film, and to the third group by a black cat in an animated film cartoon. The control group was shown no acts of aggression.

During the next twenty minutes, the children were allowed to play with a number of objects, including those the various models had used during the demonstration (doll, hammer, etc.). The result was that children in the three experimental groups showed roughly twice as much aggression as children in the control group. There was an increase not only in the number of aggressive acts similar to those that the experi-mental groups had just watched, but also in all sorts of other types of aggression. There were, moreover, slight differences

30

between the responses of the three experimental groups: while Group 1 (live model) showed a larger number of imitative acts of aggression, Group 3 (cartoon cat) produced a larger number of non-imitative acts.

Whatever view we take of these and other findings (e.g. by Mussen and Rutherford 1961; Schönbach 1967; Hartmann 1969), it is quite impossible to read any degree of catharsis into them. What they show, instead, is an increase in potential aggressiveness.

Even the possible objection that suggestion plays some part immediately after such demonstrations, but sooner or later makes way for catharsis, is refuted by empirical findings: when Hicks (1965) conducted an experiment similar to that of Bandura, Ross and Ross, he was able to show that the influence of the demonstration persisted for at least six months. There is only one possible conclusion: watching aggressive acts, far from reducing the aggressive tendency, increases it considerably.

Perhaps an experiment by Feshbach (1961) shows under what conditions the watching of aggressive scenes may nevertheless have a cathartic effect. Disgruntled students who were shown an aggressive film proved less aggressive than disgruntled students who had watched a neutral film. On the other hand, contented students who were shown an aggressive film proved to be more aggressive in the concluding test than contented students who had watched a neutral film. This suggests that the watching of aggressive scenes may have a cathartic effect on those who are in a matching emotional state (rage and anger), but not on others.

This is precisely how Buss (1961) interpreted similar experiments specially designed to investigate the psychoanalytic variant of catharsis theory, according to which those who commit overtly aggressive acts tend to repeat such acts with decreasing frequency. From this, Lorenz, like Menninger (1948) before him, concluded as late as 1963 that people should be encouraged to play sports so as to reduce their

31

tendency to engage in more serious acts of aggression.[13]

An experiment by Feshbach (1955) has long been considered clear evidence in favour of the modified catharsis hypothesis (but cf. Hokanson and Burgess 1962b). When disgruntled students were given the chance to fit what words they liked to four pictures, a questionnaire showed them to be less aggressive than disgruntled students who had not been given this chance.

But Feshbach (1956) has also demonstrated that aggressive acts have no cathartic effect in the absence of emotional stimulation. A group of children provided with 'aggressive' toys (Red Indians, tin soldiers) proved significantly more aggressive than a control group provided with trains, animals, etc. Moreover, the aggressive responses of the first group in no way gave rise to cathartic affects in subsequent situations.

Quite often aggressive acts are followed not so much by catharsis as by an increase in aggressive impulses (see Walters and Brown 1963; Little and Adams 1965, etc.). Learning experiments suggest further that the increased readiness to commit further acts of aggression after an initial one is not confined to the laboratory (see Chapter 3).

Buss's distinction, too (angry aggression has a cathartic effect; instrumental aggression has not), is probably too vague. Thus Hokanson *et al.*, having demonstrated an increase in the systolic blood pressure of experimental subjects who had been annoyed, looked for the means of reversing this process. They found that the blood pressure drops back relatively quickly in *male* students if they are allowed to attack the frustrator verbally or physically (by delivering an electric shock). The blood pressure, moreover, also drops back relatively quickly when, believing that the frustrator has a relatively high status, the students do *not* attack him.

By contrast, the blood pressure does not drop quickly if the students are able to commit aggressive acts indirectly, e.g. by telling stories. Nor does it drop back quickly if the aggression is directed against a substitute and not against the frustrator himself (Hokanson, Burgess and Cohen 1963; Gambaro and Rabin 1969). (This experiment incidentally argues strongly against the displacement hypothesis.)

In female subjects, attacked by female experimenters, the heightened blood pressure dropped back more *slowly* after aggressive than after non-aggressive responses (Hokanson *et al.*, 1968). This probably means that the blood pressure returns to normal most quickly when the subject is allowed to express what reactions to irritation he or she has learned. Since our culture generally frowns on aggressive behaviour in women, aggression does not lead to a normalization of their blood pressure. The male, by contrast, is normally allowed to indulge in open, reactive acts of aggression from childhood – hence the sudden drop in blood pressure after such acts.

In fact, the picture is much more complicated still. Holmes (1966) was unable to confirm Hokanson's first results – he discovered no catharsis. Neither did Kahn (1960) find all the expected results in incensed students, and Mallick and McCandless (1966) had similar experiences with children. But even had the results been more uniform, what would they really have proved? Simply that an effect-indicator (the blood pressure), but not aggressiveness as such, had been reduced. Now, the reduction in tension following aggressive acts is likely to lead to increased aggressiveness during future tensions.

Unsubstantiated, too, are the claims by Rosenbaum and de Charmes (1960) that the lower the self-esteem of the experimental subject the more quickly catharsis sets in; by Fishman (1965) that the subject's normal state of aggressiveness influences the cathartic effects of aggression; and by Gambaro and Rabin (1969) that the same effects are associated with guilt feelings.

All in all, therefore, the old catharsis hypothesis, on the basis of which psychoanalytically minded 'therapists' and educators feel entitled to show aggressive films to aggressive children, or encourage them to play aggressive games

33

(for the purpose of 'abreaction'), is rather outdated.

As Bandura and Walters (1964) have remarked, it is surprising that, far from applying the same technique to the reduction of sexual tensions, most educationalists (and censors) expect nothing but sexual arousal from the display of erotic films and books.

The modern attitude to catharsis may be summed up as follows:

The observation or performance of aggressive acts may reduce rage and anger in those who have previously learned to react in this way (in our society, men rather than women). The associated feeling of 'relief' from the emotional tension in its turn increases the likelihood that, in similar circumstances, these people will again want to watch or perform aggressive acts.

If aggressive acts are watched or performed without any initial feelings of rage or anger, then aggressive tendencies are likely to increase (unless punishment follows the aggressive acts there and then).

Occasionally an aggressive act may be followed by pseudo-catharsis due to exhaustion. If the act was successful, the probability of further aggression after recuperation is increased.

We might add that when research into the effects of aggression is limited to a relatively short span of time, cathartic effects tend to appear after emotionally charged acts of aggression. Long-term studies, by contrast, show that *the observation and performance of successful aggressive acts increases the probability of further aggressive acts; indeed that they may create a special need for aggressive behaviour* (see Chapter 3).

### THE F-A HYPOTHESIS AS A LONG-TERM MODEL

Dollard *et al.* first advanced F-A theory as a short-term model of aggression, but in later parts of their book (1939) they increasingly treated it as a long-term model.

34

In the short-term model, frustration is said to lead directly to aggression; in the long-term model, it is said to lead to aggression after a significant lapse of time. The long-term model suggests, for instance, that highly aggressive adults may have been frustrated, not directly before they committed an act of aggression, but in early childhood.

The long-term model calls for a redefinition of the two central concepts of the F-A hypothesis. To begin with, 'frustration' must be used in the broad sense (see page 14). Thus all unsatisfied needs (see Plack) must be treated as frustrations, including illness and accidents (Palmer). Moreover, the consequence of frustration is no longer aggression but aggressiveness, i.e. a permanent tendency or 'quality'.

Ingenious and stimulating though it undoubtedly is, the long-term model has never been put to the empirical test. Nothing is simpler than to 'prove' the existence of frustrations[14] in early childhood. There is the birth trauma, frustration of bottle feeding, bowel control and – if we are of the psychoanalytic faith – castration threats by the parents, as well as a host of others to choose from.

No one has proved that any of these are *bona fide* frustrations, or has bothered to define the 'time-fuse' effect of those alleged frustrations that occur in childhood and lead to such deplorable acts of aggression in adult life.[15]

Admittedly, if we take the trouble, we can scrape together a few findings in favour of the long-term model: part of Bandura and Walters (1959) may be made to say that aggressive youths were more frustrated in childhood than non-aggressive ones, and Palmer (1960) obtained comparable results from his studies of murderers. However, more recently, Bandura and Walters have given a different interpretation of the same data: the frustrating behaviour of their parents, and corporal punishment in particular, provide children with models of aggressive behaviour which they subsequently copy. The long-term model has also been refuted by the findings of Sears *et al.* (1953); Wittenborn (1954); and many others.

The fragility of the long-term model can therefore no longer be disguised. If Plack takes up the cudgels for greater freedom in sex education, he has good reason to do so, but this does not entitle anyone to equate sexual freedom with pacific behaviour since the two develop independently, though only a fool would claim that they do not influence each other.

## THE LONGEVITY OF THE F-A HYPOTHESIS

In view of the many weaknesses of F-A theory it is surprising to find that it should have survived for so long. The answer is far from simple. To begin with, F-A theory can very easily be incorporated into other systems – instinct theory, for instance, can treat frustration as a releaser of dammed-up aggression. Secondly, it should be remembered that the F-A hypothesis is less often advanced in serious studies of aggression than it is in popular and ideological writings.

F-A theory has the advantage of being simple and easily comprehensible, and of excusing human aggression on the grounds that it is reactive: we are only aggressive because we have been provoked (frustrated). As a long-term model, F-A theory even allows us to seek excuses in the obscure events and frustrations of early childhood: 'If I am aggressive, the fault is my parents'.' But, above all, F-A theory allows every one of us to play the amateur psychologist.

### Notes

1. On page 6 the blocking process itself is described as 'frustration'; on page 12 it is the result of such interference that is so described.
2. We say 'relatively', because although Dollard's formulations are much clearer than Freud's (in all his writings Freud made no attempt to define 'aggression'), they leave a great many

problems unsolved, a failure that Buss, in particular, has tried to remedy.

3. If a German nine-year-old has relatively free access to television, and watches it for about two hours a day, he will observe more than four major acts of aggression every day (data compiled by Fräulein Gebhardt and Frau Lange of the Technical University, Brunswick). By the time he is fifteen, he will have witnessed more than 14,000 acts of violent assault, manslaughter and murder. Can anyone seriously suggest that this has no effect on the child's general attitude?

4. Sears *et al.* (1957); Feshbach (1964) and Loy and Turnbull (1964) take a similar view. Berkowitz (1962, p. 43), however, adds that fear or anxiety may be further emotional reactions to frustration.

5. These models were accomplices of the experimenter.

6. There seems little point in basing aggression on special mechanisms. We might equally well introduce special mechanisms for dependency and sexual behaviour, in which case we should be doing precisely what so many psychologists tried to do at the beginning of the century, namely to solve the problems by compiling long lists of instincts or drives.

7. The 'hand-test' (Belschner, Lischke and Selg 1971) was designed to measure aggressiveness (see Selg 1968). The subjects are presented with thirty-four small photographs of a hand and are asked what that hand might be doing. The most commonly used indicator of aggressiveness is the AOS (acting-out score), $\Sigma$ (agg + dir) − (aff + dep + com + fear), where:

agg = aggression (determined from such answers as 'the hand is slapping somebody');

dir = direct answers such as 'the hand is directing someone forward';

aff = expression of positive feelings such as 'the hand is waving at a friend';

dep = dependence; such answers as 'the hand is asking for help';

com = communication; such answers as 'the hand is signalling to somebody';

fear = such answers as 'the hand of a frightened man'.

8. See n. 7 above.

9. cf. Kregarman and Worchel (1961); Fishman (1965); Mallick and McCandless (1966).

37

10. On this assumption it is difficult to explain why so many hangmen take their own lives that suicide may be called their professional hazard (K. Rossa, quoted in *Der Spiegel*, No. 45, 1966).

11. We should like to remind the reader that even the optimal use of vision has to be learned during childhood. Hebb (1967, p. 178) reports that a girl born with a cataract and cured by surgery in late adolescence quickly learned to distinguish between colours, but could never recognize more than three persons apart by sight alone.

    Animal experiments have confirmed the importance of the learning, during the first few years of life, of many types of behaviour that were previously considered much more genetically determined, e.g. sexual behaviour and the rearing of offspring (see Harlow and Harlow 1961).

12. Correlation co-efficients range between $+1.00$ and $-1.00$. If the assumption of F-A theory was correct, i.e. that outward and inward aggression can replace each other, the correlations would tend to be negative.

13. Lorenz could not have been very familiar with such popular 'jousting games' as football, which far too frequently involve deliberate fouls and acts of vandalism on the part of the spectators. He could not, of course, have known in 1963 that a football match would become the prelude to a war (between El Salvador and Honduras in 1970).

14. Those who do so, e.g. the psychoanalytically schooled philosopher Plack, usually ignore the empirical refutations by Orlans or others.

15. An incomplete proof is found in Berkowitz (1962).

*Ute Jakobi, Herbert Selg and
Wilfried Belschner*

# 2. THE AGGRESSIVE INSTINCT

## 2. THE AGGRESSIVE INSTINCT

### 1. Drive, instinct and motivation

In German-speaking countries there have been countless attempts to base human aggression on the existence of a special instinct or drive. The best-known advocates of this approach are Freud and Lorenz. Before we examine the ideas of two such famous though controversial men, we must first say a few words about 'drive', 'instinct' and 'motivation'.

*Motivation:* Hofstätter (1957b, p. 53) advises his readers to speak of human motives rather than of human drives, and this is, in fact, the approach of a great many modern psychologists. In other words the 'Why?' of human behaviour is best answered by a complex motivational analysis.

*Drive and instinct:* English translators of German authors generally translate the German *Trieb* indifferently as 'drive' or 'instinct', though 'drive' is less specific than *Trieb*. 'Drive' is chiefly applied to inner tension and often designates no more than a general state of excitation or activation without a specific content or goal. 'Instinct', by contrast, is usually applied to relatively organized, inherited and innate behaviour schemata. This concept is narrower than the

41

German *Trieb*, and is generally used in English discussions of Freudian ideas.

It has often been asked whether man has instincts at all, and if so, how many. The instinct most easily demonstrated is the sucking reflex: an infant who has not been suckled for some time becomes agitated (appetitive behaviour in the broadest sense), and if his mother applies her nipple to his lips, this 'releaser' triggers off the acceptance of the nipple, followed by sucking, swallowing, etc.

## 2. Freud's instinct theory

Freud's 'instinct' theory underwent a great many changes over the course of time. As he himself explained (1930, p. 94): 'The whole of analytic theory has evolved gradually enough, but the theory of instincts has groped its way forward under greater difficulties than any other part of it.' Just how difficult this advance proved to be may be gathered from the following, later, quotation (1933, p. 101):

> The theory of instincts is, as it were, our mythology. The instincts are mythical beings, superb in their indefiniteness. In our work, we cannot for a moment overlook them and yet we are never certain that we are seeing them clearly. You know how popular thought deals with instincts. It postulates as many different instincts as may be needed – an instinct of assertiveness, instincts of imitation and of play, a social instinct, and a great many more besides. It takes them up, as it were, lets each do its particular work, and then drops them again. We have always suspected that behind this multitude of small, occasional instincts there lies something much more serious and powerful, which must be approached with circumspection.

42

Freud put forward a dual theory in which two 'primitive forces', the life and death instincts, opposed each other. But what precisely was an instinct? According to the later Freud, to whom the death instinct became increasingly important, instincts are 'the forces we assume to exist behind the tensions of the Id (i.e. behind the vital layer). They are the body's demands on psychic life' (1938, p. 70). And though they are the final cause of all activity, they have a conservative character, i.e. they tend to restore the past. All have a source, an impetus, an aim and an object (1905b).

## THE SOURCE

The source of an instinct, according to Freud, is 'that somatic process in an organ or part of the body whose stimulus is represented by the instinct in psychic life'. He added that it was unknown whether this process was purely chemical or whether it might not be mechanical as well. The study of instinctual sources, Freud continued (1915a, p. 215) was not really part of, or essential to, psychological research. Though its somatic origins gave the instinct its characteristic stamp, the instinct itself could only be identified by its psychological goal. This later saved Freud the trouble of having to isolate the instinctual source of instincts – though he referred briefly to the somatic sources of the life instinct (1938, p. 73), he did not think it necessary to name the source of the death instinct.

## THE IMPETUS

Instincts have a characteristic impetus, i.e. a characteristic amount of force. 'It seems . . . that an instinct is a compulsion inherent in organic life to restore an earlier state of things' (1920, p. 38).

43

## THE AIM

The aim of an instinct is *satisfaction* which 'can only be obtained by abolishing the condition of stimulation in the source of the instinct'. Or, as he put it in an earlier text (1905b), 'We may say that the aim of an instinct is the action it dictates' (e.g. coitus).

## THE OBJECT

The object of an instinct is 'that in or through which it can achieve its aim. It is the most variable thing about an instinct and is not originally connected with it, but becomes attached to it only in consequence of being peculiarly fitted to provide satisfaction. The object is not necessarily an extraneous one: it may be part of the subject's own body. It may be changed any number of times, and this capacity for change plays an important part in the life of the individual' (1915a, p. 215). In the sexual instinct of the normal adult, 'the sexual object is that person from whom the sexual attraction emanates' (1905b).

## FURTHER CHARACTERISTICS OF INSTINCTS

Freud kept stressing the fact that instincts occupy a borderline position between the psychic and the somatic spheres.

Instincts differ from external stimuli in that they have a constant effect from which it is impossible to escape. The two types of instinct (death instincts, life instincts) rarely if ever appear separately; they are mixed in varying proportions and cannot be completely isolated. The total separation of instincts is confined to the pathological realm (neurosis, psychosis).

## DEATH INSTINCT, DESTRUCTIVE INSTINCT AND AGGRESSIVE INSTINCT

Freud's last formulation of the dualistic approach, which appeared in 1920 and to which he kept harking back in later years, represents the end of a long struggle to develop a theory in which human aggression played some part from the very outset. Until 1920, Freud had been unhappy about the existence of an independent aggressive instinct. 'In spite of all the uncertainty and obscurity of our theory of instincts, I should prefer for the present to adhere to the usual view, which leaves each instinct its own power of becoming aggressive,' Freud explained in 1909 (p. 372).

The First World War drew Freud's attention increasingly to the phenomenon of aggression, as witness his *Thoughts for the Times on War and Death* (1915). He took the decisive step in 1920 with his distinction between an independent death (destructive) instinct and a life instinct (Eros). He fully appreciated the speculative character of this distinction, but what started out as a working hypothesis eventually became an integral part of his general theory.

According to Freud, the death instinct must always be considered in conjunction with the life instinct. The life instinct, which strives to preserve the living substance and to combine it into ever larger units, and the death instinct, which tries to destroy these units and to restore the original, inorganic state, always appear side by side and complement each other (1930). The primary task and aim of the death instinct (or the destructive instinct, as Freud called it) is to change the quick into the dead. Relying on the analogy of the physiological process of anabolism and katabolism, Freud held the death instinct responsible for disintegration or separation, and the life instinct for cohesion and fusion and hence the continuance of life. The collaboration of, and the conflict between, these two instincts was said to hold the secret to the phenomenon of life.

45

But having defined the general *aim* of the death instinct, Freud still had to determine its *source*, and the fact that he failed to do so may be called the crucial flaw in his model. Almost by way of an excuse, he explained that the fate of the libido (the energy of the life instinct) was much simpler to follow (1930). The 'silent' death instinct only speaks to us when it manifests itself in the form of the destructive instinct. In general, we can merely divine its existence behind Eros; it would elude us completely were it not fused with the latter (1930). A total separation of the two is very rare – we meet it in those psychotics or neurotics who carry self-destruction to the point of suicide (1925; 1938).

As Freud pointed out elsewhere (1924), Eros helps the living organism to render the death instinct 'harmless' by externalization, i.e. by projecting it on to objects outside the self. Since all life is a state of tension ending in death, the death instinct must win out in the long run, even though Eros, by propagating new life, keeps notching up minor victories. If the death instinct were not repeatedly deflected from its aim – the reduction of tension or excitation through self-destruction – by the life instinct, then death would not keep individuals waiting long. Crucial to the survival of the individual, therefore, is the transfer of the self-destructive tendency inherent in the death instinct to an outward form of motor aggression. All the energy of the death instinct that cannot be deflected on to outside objects remains directed against the self.

Freud often used the terms 'death' and 'destructive' instinct as synonyms, though, in 1923, he introduced a distinction between the two, based on direction (inward or outward). For Freud 'aggression' was, to all intents and purposes, equivalent to destruction: the aggressive instinct was the 'derivative and main representative of the death instinct' (1930). He never attempted to provide a definition of aggression, preferring to treat it, like all instincts, as a 'mythical being'.

INHIBITION, DISPLACEMENT, SUBLIMATION
AND CATHARSIS

In what follows we shall briefly examine what Freud thought of the inhibition, displacement, sublimation and cathartic effects of aggression. It cannot, however, be stressed strongly enough that, because of the fusion of life and death instincts, Freud found it most difficult to trace the vicissitudes of either.

*Inhibition*

To Freud, the inhibition of aggression was a crucial phenomenon in the lives of individuals no less than of societies. The greater the inhibition of external aggression, the greater and more self-destructive the self-directed aggression (1923). This was particularly true of the cultural repression of instincts (1924). The suppression of other-directed aggression helps the super-ego (the conscience) to produce guilt feelings which become greater the more an individual refrains from aggressive acts against others. In other words, Freud did not postulate an original or primary form of morality responsible for instinctual renunciation, but held that it was instinctual renunciation (imposed by external forces) which created morality in the form of conscience. Because of man's natural temptation to vent his aggression on his neighbour, civilization has to keep aggression within bounds or face collapse (1930). Now, according to Freud, the most effective method of checking the aggressive instinct is the introjection, i.e. the internalization, of aggression, which helps the conscience to exert the same pressure on the self as the self would like to exert on others. The resulting guilt feelings express themselves as a longing for punishment. To answer the fateful question of 'how the greatest obstacle in the path of civilization, man's constitutional tendency to behave aggressively towards his fellow men, can be removed', Freud examined the commandment

'Thou shalt love thy neighbour as thyself' and called it a prime example of the unpsychological approach applied by the cultural super-ego – it is impossible to obey. Freud himself refused to prophesy whether and to what extent culture will gain the upper hand over man's aggressive and self-destructive instincts; he merely expressed the hope that Eros would make great 'efforts' to prevail over the death instinct. He thought it impossible to suppress aggression altogether, the more so as some aggression was essential to human survival. The main task of the educator is to deflect aggression so that it does not give rise to bloody wars.

In his letter to Einstein (1933b), Freud stressed the essential role of both instincts in man's life. The outward deflection of the destructive instinct plays an essential role in the life of the individual and exaggerated internalization of aggression by instinctual repression is of doubtful value. Freud greatly preferred such indirect methods of reducing extreme outward aggression as the establishment of alliances, love relationships, and so on.

### Displacement and sublimation

The displacement of aggression (from the outside to the self) is generally based on the fact that 'whenever a drive is blocked it seeks and obtains satisfaction from a substitute object' (Toman, 1954, p. 43). In Freud's view, the erotic instinct is more plastic and yielding in this respect than the destructive instinct, but he also mentions the case of neurotic revenge, in which the aggression is directed against the 'wrong' person.

In general, Freud treated displacement and its counterpart, sublimation, almost exclusively by reference to the libido model, on the grounds that the analysis of instinctual impulses shows us 'over and over again' that they are 'derivatives of Eros' (1923). In other words, he hardly touched upon the sublimation of aggression, i.e. on the way in which the aggressive energy can be diverted into culturally desirable channels.

## *Catharsis*

So much attention has been paid to catharsis in discussions of aggression (see Chapter 1) that we have to re-examine Freud's model in the light of that concept. Starting from the idea of a reduction in tension (the aim of all instincts is the reduction of organic tension by the restoration of an earlier state), many students (e.g. Berkowitz 1962) believe that, to Freud, 'catharsis' was part of his general conception of aggression – Freud thought it was possible to deflect and reduce the inner reservoir of aggressive energy by means of aggressive actions. To the best of the present writers' knowledge, however, Freud himself established no such direct connection between catharsis and aggression. This link must rather be traced back to Dollard *et al.* (see Chapter 1) who, though strongly influenced by psychoanalytical ideas, failed to acknowledge their sources.

## 3. The instinctual model of aggression in more recent psychoanalytical literature

Freud's instinct theory was given a mixed reception even in his lifetime. Only a very few psychoanalysts were able to adopt his speculative and probably subjective (cf. Jones, Book III) assumption of a death instinct, and Freud himself only did so after overcoming considerable inner resistances.

By and large, we agree with Buss (1961) that psycho-analysts can be divided into three camps. First, there is a small group which accepts Freud's death instinct with minor or major modifications (Nunberg, Menninger, Melanie Klein, and possibly Waelder). Secondly, there is a larger group which, though granting the existence of an independent aggressive instinct, does not derive it from a death instinct (this group includes Hartmann, Kris and Lowenstein, and, to some extent, Mitscherlich). Finally, there is a third group which totally rejects Freud's attempt to treat aggression as a special entity, and considers it to be a purely reactive phenomenon (Fenichel, Horney *et al.*).

### HARTMANN, KRIS AND LOEWENSTEIN

Most important to our own argument is the second group. Hartmann, Kris and Loewenstein (1949) do not – as we have said – share Freud's metaphysical conception of a death instinct, but postulate an independent aggressive instinct. Inasmuch as they use the term 'aggression' to designate both the instinct and also its energy, they have greatly added to the conceptual confusion.

They dwell at some length on the sublimation of aggression, a process to which Freud himself paid scant attention. The sublimation of aggression, they claim, plays a more important role in psychic life than does even the libido – aggressive energies are potentially so dangerous that their neutralization takes precedence over everything else. Neutralized aggression supplies the ego with the energy it needs for motor activities, including a possible retransformation into aggression. The model constructed by Hartmann *et al.* differs essentially from Freud's: while Freud believed that primary aggression is self-directed, Hartmann *et al.* contend that self-destructive impulses are a consequence of the internalization of aggression.

### MITSCHERLICH

A. Mitscherlich, the best-known German exponent of modern psychoanalysis, has devoted a great deal of attention to human aggressiveness during the past few years. In so doing he has tried to avoid any special bias: while repeatedly stressing his allegiance to the Freudian model, he doubts whether the 'death instinct is, in fact, the nuclear part of aggression' (1969c, p. 116), the more so as it does not, apparently, lend itself to empirical verification.

Mitscherlich's lack of bias is, however, somewhat spurious, for ultimately he, too, reduces aggression to an instinct. Indeed, he has (p. 82) argued that Freud's instinct theory may be considered legitimate until such time as another anthropological concept enables us to describe instinctual behaviour more concisely. Let us anticipate our own critique (see Chapter 3): anyone who is so prejudiced against learning theory that he can write that all learning involves aversion (p. 117), cannot be considered an objective witness.

Mitscherlich has added no truly original ideas to the aggression controversy. His merit lies in another plane, particularly in his courageous political commitment, and in his determination to speak out on pressing everyday problems.


## 4. Lorenz's model

### THE AGGRESSIVE INSTINCT

In his *On Aggression* (1966), Lorenz defines aggression as 'the fighting instinct in beast and man which is directed *against* members of the same species', and goes on to claim that 'aggression . . . is an instinct like any other, and in natural conditions it helps just as much as any other to ensure the survival of the individual and the species' (p. ix f.). In other words, he confines 'aggression' to intraspecific disputes – disputes between animals of different species are separated as 'interspecific fights'.

Besides aggression there are only three other 'big' instincts, namely feeding, reproduction and escape. They command a host of 'small servants' such as running, flying, etc., the so-called 'tool activities'.

Lorenz attaches four main functions to the aggressive instinct or drive, whose combined activities help to preserve the species:

(1) Thanks to (intraspecific) aggression, members of one and the same species spread out across the available territory in such a way that the chances of finding food, etc., are optimal;

(2) Rival fights between members of one and the same species serve to select the strongest for breeding and for defence against external enemies.

(3) Aggression has the further function of selecting strong 'brood defenders'. 'Among sticklebacks it is the male ... in many gallinaceous birds it is only the female which tends the brood, and which is often far more aggressive than the male.' 'The same thing is said to be true of human beings,' Lorenz adds (p. 34).

(4) Aggression helps to maintain a ranking order and thus to reduce intraspecific fights, the more so as a high-ranking animal will often protect a low-ranking one.

Aggression is not expressed just as soon as enough energy is available, for an instinctive act depends on the presence of eliciting stimuli. The longer an instinct remains unsatisfied, the more intense the organism's search for the latter (appetitive behaviour). In extreme cases, an instinct can 'explode' without demonstrable external stimuli. As an illustration, Lorenz mentions a hand-reared starling that went through the entire process of insect-eating in the absence of any kind of insect.

In Lorenz's view, man, like so many animals, has an aggressive drive, and one, moreover, that has hypertrophied – primitive man had an aggressive instinct bred into him, but the civilized life we are now forced to live prevents the spontaneous discharge of aggressive energy.

Lorenz thinks that aggressive impulses ought to be 'lived

out' if man is to preserve his mental and physical health, and in support of this view he tells us what the psychoanalyst Sydney Margolin has to say about the Ute Indians (p. 341). Environmental pressures had seemingly forced this tribe to develop an extraordinary degree of aggression within only a few centuries. Such instincts cannot possibly be satisfied in the modern world, and as a result, runs Margolin's thesis, the percentage of neurotics among the Ute has become higher than in any other human group; moreover, their 'rate of motor accidents exceeds that of any other car-driving human group' (p. 211).

## INHIBITION AND CONTROL OF AGGRESSION

According to Lorenz, a fight between wolves terminates when the weaker makes a submission gesture towards the stronger by presenting his unprotected neck. The stronger does not bite; innate inhibitions prevent it from continuing the fight.

Lorenz believes that man has inherited the same inhibitions, but that the invention of weapons has helped to suppress the inhibitory mechanism. The speed with which one armed man can kill another prevents the timely display of submission or appeasement gestures. As for remote-control weapons, they obviate all contact between the attacker and his victim so that submissive gestures cannot even be perceived. 'No sane man would even go rabbit-hunting for pleasure if the necessity of killing his prey with his natural weapons (teeth and nails) brought home to him the full emotional realization of what he is actually doing' (p. 208).

Lorenz then gives a series of behavioural prescriptions for reducing the dangers posed by our hypertrophied aggressive instinct. To begin with, intraspecific aggression can be redirected at substitute objects: we can, for instance, chop wood rather than kick an opponent. (Lorenz obviously fails to distinguish between displacement, sublimation and catharsis;

53

p. 240 f.) He considers sport to be a particularly human form of redirected aggression. Much as many animals engage in 'ritual fighting', so man's aggressive drive can be satisfied by competitive sports. Moreover, sport unites human beings by bonds of personal friendship, and personal friendship between members of different nations reduces the danger of war. No man can unreservedly hate a nation several members of which he counts among his friends (p. 224). Enthusiasm, too – for art or science, for instance – must be considered a sublimation of aggression, and laughter, finally, creates a 'strong fellow-feeling' among men: 'Laughing men hardly ever shoot!' (p. 254).

### 5. Critique of Lorenz's model

The problem of whether or not human aggressiveness can be traced back to an instinct or drive is not a purely academic one – the answer has important socio-political repercussions. If aggressiveness is a constant flow of instinctual energy, then we must take good care to channel it. We must learn to redirect and dam it up in time, and so keep the damage down to a minimum, or even derive some benefit from the dammed-up energy. On the other hand, if aggressive behaviour is learned, then we must try to prevent the learning of violent forms of aggression and to encourage the learning of co-operative behaviour.

The fact that aggression had to be learned would not mean that it is created *ex nihilo* (as Mitscherlich concluded quite illogically; see *Publik* of 4 September 1970); all learned behaviour is based on man's activity, on his successes and failures (see Chapter 3) and on the opportunities he has of imitating others.

Basically, all instinct theories suffer from the fact that they label rather than explain behaviour patterns. We watch an affray, classify it as an aggression and trace it back to an aggressive instinct, a death instinct, a *mortido* or *destrudo* (cf. Mitscherlich 1969, p. 83), or what you will. Many seem satisfied with the resulting jingle of sounds. But, in this way, it is possible to set up lists of instincts as long as we like; there is no criterion for closing such lists. Freud made a fetish of the number two – he stuck to his dualistic instinct system come what may. Lorenz has adopted four instincts; McDougall eighteen; Bernard is said to have opted for 14,046 (Dorsch, p. 159).

It seems reasonable that, if we are prepared to accept a large number of instincts, we ought also to grant the existence of several aggressive instincts, for it seems rather unsatisfactory to combine the aggressive acts of a sadistic murderer or a Hitler with the verbal aggression of a day-dreaming neurotic. Instinct-theorists cannot offer a satisfactory explanation of the multiplicity of aggressive outbursts and of their situational characteristics by reference to a single instinct. Moreover, they have not yet been able to locate the somatic source of the alleged aggressive instinct or to specify the resulting stimuli. Releasers of instinctual actions – and no one knows this better than Lorenz – can be described fairly accurately. In man, however, almost any stimulus whatsoever can release aggression. And what precisely is the human instinctive *action* labelled 'aggression'? Why, when dealing with the human aggressive instinct in particular, is it almost impossible to adduce two identical acts of aggression?

Instinct theorists generally follow Freud in immunizing themselves against all such objections by refusing to specify what they mean by aggression, or else they follow Lorenz and supply a non-definition: aggression is a fighting instinct directed at a member of one's species.

Does the ubiquity of human aggression, or the fact that even small children show aggression, prove the existence of an aggressive instinct? The ubiquity merely proves that, wherever men may live, aggressive acts lead to success. As for the early age at which children show aggression, it must be stressed that, at the same age, they have learned many other behaviour patterns as well: they can utter a few words, lift up objects, etc. Must we describe everything the infant does as an instinct? In that case we should also have to speak of a nose-picking instinct, for nose-picking is another universal phenomenon that appears early on in the individual's life.

We have no wish to repeat every criticism that has been levelled at the instinct model (for a more detailed discussion, the reader is referred to Berkowitz, Buss and Dann). Freud, as we realize today, was 'only' a child of his time. The reasons why sexuality and aggressiveness forced themselves upon his attention as dominant classes of behaviour were, in the first case, because he lived in Vienna at the turn of the century, and, in the second case, because of the shock of the First World War.

The Second World War was more horrible still, so much so that, for years, science preferred to say nothing at all on the subject of human aggressiveness, possibly because scientists themselves were riddled with guilt. Not until some fifteen years after the war's end did the discussion revive. In Germany, Lorenz rose to prominence. His critics objected, quite early on, that his views of aggression seemed to provide an excuse for a great many whose own reputation was not entirely unblemished, and who could now argue that no one should blame them for having expressed what was, after all, a basic human instinct.

Lorenz's popularity was further enhanced by the fact that most people tend to respect the dicta of authorities. Now Lorenz is not only an authority on animal behaviour but also likes to quote the great poets, and while reciting Goethe may not be the best scientific method, it has an undoubted aesthetic appeal. In addition, Lorenz has a vast stock of popular sayings. (These are always convincing, even though many people may use 'many hands make light work' as well as 'too many cooks spoil the broth' without noticing the contradiction.) Moreover, he has an attractive style, though he is sometimes carried away by his own eloquence: when he argues that in man, too, the brood-tending parent is more aggressive than the other, he may elicit a chuckle from many a *pater familias;* for the rest he flies in the face of psychological experience.

It is time to speak plainly: neither the ethologist Lorenz nor the psychoanalyst Mitscherlich knows very much about the psychology of human aggression, their own claims to the contrary notwithstanding. Both conveniently ignore whatever does not fit into their theories.

Let us, for instance, look at the modern psychologists that Mitscherlich acknowledges in his *Aggression und Anpassung* (an essay that has been reprinted on three separate occasions): apart from Lorenz, Sigmund and Anna Freud, he refers to a handful of other 'depth psychologists' – and that is all. There is not a single reference to the pioneering studies of Bandura, Walters, Berkowitz or Buss.

Lorenz's 'psychology' is refuted more easily still. It might be called a kind of private science, were not every science a subject of public concern. He likes to quote Goethe, Schiller and the Bible, and the only psychologist he cites at some length in *On Aggression* is the 'psychiatrist and psycho-analyst' Sydney Margolin, who is said to have made 'very exact' studies of Prairie Indians (the Ute Indians, see page 210 of Lorenz's book). Now this claim is quite unsupported, for, as Montagu (1968) points out, Margolin has published no verifiable data (cf. Steward, p. 105). For the rest, the Ute are not Prairie Indians, as Lorenz claims, not are they conspicuously aggressive, forced to commit suicide after killing fellow tribesmen, or distinguished by suffering a larger number of road accidents than other human groups, etc. Hence it is not even worth bothering to ask how Margolin or Lorenz established that the Ute have a greater tendency to succumb to neuroses or accidents than anyone else.

Perhaps we ought merely to smile when an ethologist makes untenable assertions about the human psyche. But it is astonishing to find how many of his fellow ethologists have given the lie even to Lorenz's descriptions of animal behaviour. Those of his colleagues who have collaborated in Montagu's book accuse him, *inter alia*, of misrepresenting our nearest relatives, the apes – these animals are friendly, not aggressive. Even Lorenz's accounts of fights between rats have been referred to by Barnett (p. 20) as fables.[1]

How seriously are we to take Lorenz's claim that laughing men hardly ever shoot? Has he, who believes that no man can kill a hare with his bare hands, read no reports about life in concentration camps? Might we not equally well conclude that writing men do not shoot; that drivers do not shoot; that flirts do not shoot, etc? One psychologist has claimed that Lorenz's book is, in fact, a satire, and that its place is not beside works on psychology but beside those written by the lesser descendants of Jonathan Swift.

**Note**

1. Since instincts are species-specific, it is quite impermissible to argue from animal to human instincts, or to create man in the image of a few fishes and birds.

*Wilfried Belschner*

# 3. LEARNING AND AGGRESSION

# 3. LEARNING AND AGGRESSION[1]

## 1. Aggression-specific models as social conventions

Does the fact that 2·17 million crimes were recorded in Federal Germany during 1969, that not a single year passes without one war or another, and that so many acts occur of individual and collective aggression, bear out the F-A hypothesis of the existence of an aggressive instinct? And must we conclude further that aggression is part of man's very 'essence', a deep need demanding satisfaction?

Both the F-A and the instinct models assume that aggressive behaviour is governed by specific rules which set it off from all other forms of behaviour. But, in that case, are we not equally entitled to construct, say, a frustration-resignation hypothesis, a frustration-escape hypothesis, etc.? And why do Freudians postulate the existence of no more than two drives or instincts – albeit for purely pragmatic reasons?

One answer might be that belief in the necessity of aggressive behaviour has become a cultural truism (Hofstätter 1957), so much so that the use of threats and force is accepted as a group norm. And it can easily be shown in other spheres – that of sex-specific norms, for instance – that every group tends to treat its truisms as biological facts. Thus, much as

61

Westermarck (quoted in Hofstätter 1957) saw fit to speak of a 'monogamous instinct', many recent writers have taken it for granted that something as obvious and natural as aggression must also be bound up with an inner drive. Society has an ambivalent attitude to aggression: while it condemns its disturbing features, it also claims that it is 'useful' (e.g. in preserving the species; Lorenz 1964) and 'natural'.

From these remarks it should be clear that the increased attention currently being paid to aggression is a cultural trend; and that the treatment of aggression as part of the class of instinct-determined forms of behaviour is based on a general consensus (Hofstätter 1957); for that reason, such treatment must be considered a mere convention.

## 2. Non-aggression and international relations

Those who share the view presented in the preceding section will look upon aggressive acts as forms of social behaviour produced and changed by environmental circumstances. In that case it ought to be possible to determine under what conditions aggressive behaviour appears, persists or vanishes.

This approach has a considerable bearing on international relations. Is it purely Utopian to speak of a social system based on peaceful attitudes? Or must we put a good face on the existence of a characteristic 'aggressive faculty' (Mitscherlich 1969b), and see the main task of individual and social education in the channelling and 'attenuation' of this 'easily aroused psychological need of man' (Mitscherlich 1969b)?

If Mitscherlich and like-minded psychoanalysts are right, then we must resign ourselves to living under a perpetual threat. We must, for instance, accept the paradoxical behaviour of politicians who mouth peace even while doing their utmost to increase their country's 'overkill capacity', who believe wholeheartedly in *si vis pacem, para bellum*.

62

From Hegel's dictum that revolutionary ideas shake reality, it follows that the first step in the development of peaceful behaviour must be the rejection of the thought patterns inherent in instinct theory.

In its stead, we need not postulate that man is 'naturally peaceful', a view that Mitscherlich (1969b) rightly calls an illusion, but simply that man is 'naturally plastic', i.e. that he learns his characteristic behaviour patterns in the course of his socialization. We accordingly maintain that human institutions are responsible for the social actions man performs and for the norms adopted by his group. It is only in this way that we can hope to break out of the following vicious circle:

Postulate of an aggressive instinct → search for aggressive behaviour patterns → interpretation of concrete behaviour patterns as expressions of the aggressive instinct (possibly in sublimated form) → *a posteriori* deduction of an aggressive instinct from the recurrence of these 'aggressive' acts.

With the Hegelian approach, by contrast, we start out by granting the possibility of aggression-free human beings.[2] In that case, we must also assume that the learning and implementation of aggressive behaviour patterns depend on specific environmental factors, and that man is capable of solving his conflicts in more than one way.

To determine the statistical distribution of 'aggressiveness', we use the same normal distribution[3] that we usually apply to other characteristic personal attributes. The most important consequence is that individuals with an 'abnormally' low degree of aggression are not immediately classified as psychopathological deviants (suffering from 'neurosis', 'repression', or 'inhibition').

The importance of this approach becomes particularly obvious in the sphere of international relations. Among the psychological conditions of peace, Bergius (1967) mentions the expectation that peace is possible. In the United States, for instance, it was shown that the issuing of air defence handbooks served as an official endorsement of the belief that a nuclear war was probable, which greatly increased the (subjective) probability of its outbreak (Nowak and Lerner 1960). Similarly, the belief that aggression-specific mechanisms have a biological basis must also increase the subjective probability of the occurrence of aggressive acts.

In this essay, I shall attempt to specify several of the conditions in which the development of aggression – if treated as a learned form of social behaviour – can be guided and controlled. For, 'since wars begin in the minds of men, it is in the minds of men that the defences of peace must be constructed' (UNESCO Charter).

## 3. Application of learning theory to aggressive behaviour

Aggression is a highly complex type of social behaviour. For a discussion of the methodological problems involved in social learning (e.g. what operational definition should be adopted for the behaviour patterns to be learned or for the comparison of molar behaviour units) the reader is referred to Chapter 5.

### THREE LEARNING CONCEPTS: CLASSICAL CONDITIONING, OPERANT CONDITIONING AND IMITATION OF MODELS

Three models have proved particularly useful in the interpretation of learning processes: (a) classical conditioning (Pavlov from about 1900; Watson 1914); (b) operant conditioning (Skinner 1938; Hull 1943), also called 'instrumental conditioning' or 'learning through success'; and (c) learning through imitation (Bandura and Walters 1963; Bandura 1968), also called 'learning through observation', and 'learning through identification (with a model)'.

Assuming that aggressive tendencies are learned, we are

entitled to ask two questions. What, first of all, is the significance of each of these three models in the study of aggression? (As far as the author knows, the literature contains no experiments based on classical conditioning, except for the hypnotic experiments of Barendregt (1969).) Secondly, what happens during the learning of aggressive behaviour patterns?

## 4. Operant conditioning

SUCCESS THROUGH AGGRESSIVE BEHAVIOUR

Let us start with the operant-conditioning model illustrated in Figure 3.

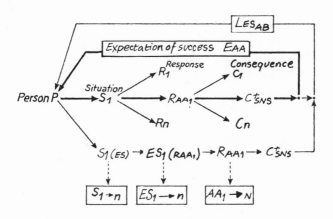

Fig 3  Operant conditioning of aggressive behaviour

A hungry boy named John passes a fruit stall and gets away with stealing an apple. The apple is delicious and filling.

In this example the boy's general situation $S_1$ can be described by his unsatisfactory inner state (hunger) and certain characteristics of his external situation (fruit stall).

The general situation, $S_1$, might have served as a cue for a host of different actions ($R_1 \rightarrow R_n$): John might have bought food in a grocer's shop ($R_1$), have gone home ($R_2$), and so on ($R_n$). The aggressive action ($R_{AA1}$) he chose for whatever reasons brought him success (positive consequence $C^+$) in two respects: it led to the elimination of the unsatisfactory inner state, and it also ensured social 'success' in the boy's contact with the stallholder. John may have broken the social rules, but he was not caught.

Thorndike's 'law of effect' (1913) enables us to make the following prognosis: since the first aggressive act ($R_{AA1}$) has proved successful, the probability of similar responses in situations resembling $S_1$ (hunger, fruit stall) is increased. Success with an aggressive action ($S_{AA}$) will thus, in time, lead to an observable contraction of behavioural responses. (For a detailed discussion of Thorndike's law, see Blöschl (1969); Foppa (1965).)

The inner state of the person and the situational characteristics act as 'stimuli' on the behaviour (responses) of that person and determine whether or not such behaviour is felt to be successful.

Thus if John had been caught stealing by the stallholder, or if the stolen apple had been rotten, he would have been dissatisfied with both the social and the individual aspects of his action. In that case, his action would not have received positive reinforcement ($C^+$), and the likelihood of further aggressive actions in the general situation $S_1$ would have decreased. Lack of success thus leads to the 'extinction' of a given behaviour pattern.

In our example, hunger was said to have impelled the boy to act aggressively. If we consider other circumstances, we find that, in man, such physiological or 'primary' needs as hunger and thirst are not the only 'motors' of aggressive behaviour – there is also a whole series of non-physiological or 'secondary' motives, such as a thirst for power, position, etc., all of which had to be 'learned'.

## 'EXPECTATION OF SUCCESS THROUGH AGGRESSIVE BEHAVIOUR' AS A SECONDARY MOTIVE

As everyone knows from his own experience, aggression is a remarkably effective means of changing reality. Thus threats or the use of force often help us to get our own way with minimum delay. More generally, we can say that, in the cultural climate we inhabit, aggressive behaviour has a high probability of satisfying a large variety of needs.

A crucial element in the emergence of aggressive behaviour is therefore the expectation that it will be crowned with success ($ES_{AB}$).

Let us return to our example. Assume that the apple was the first thing John ever stole, in which case his initial chances of success or failure might be put at 50:50. He may well tell himself it was sheer 'luck' that he got away with it. Now let us assume that he continues to still his hunger in the same way. Repeated success is likely to lead to a change in his expectations:

| Number of successful thefts | 1 | 2 | 3 | 4 | 5 | 6 | 7 | ... | n |
|---|---|---|---|---|---|---|---|---|---|
| Prior estimate of successful outcome | 50:50 | 55:45 | 55:45 | 60:40 | 70:30 | 80:20 | 80:20 | ... | 100:0 |

In the above illustration, we have assumed a gradual change in the respective estimates of success from 50:50 (the figures might equally well have been 40:60) to 100:0.

The more probable the successful outcome, the greater the expectation of gaining satisfaction by means of aggressive acts.

If, following Norbert Wiener (1952), we define learning as a form of 'feedback', i.e. 'a method of controlling a system by reinserting into it the results of its past performance', then we can advance the following hypothesis: the repeated success of aggressive actions helps to build a lasting 'expectation of success through aggressive behaviour ($ES_{AB}$)'. In other words, a person can 'learn' to expect success ($LES_{AB}$; see Figure 3) in situations with specific characteristics.

Again, if someone has been relatively unsuccessful with other social attitudes, e.g. with 'expectation of success through peaceful conduct', then $ES_{AB}$ may still appeal to him as a secondary form of behaviour and help to determine his selection of behavioural responses in specific situations.

## THE AGGRESSIVE CYCLE

The close links between specific situation, confirmed expectations of success, aggressive behaviour and need satisfaction, may lead to the suppression of other, non-aggressive, forms of behaviour ($R_1 \rightarrow R_n$), i.e. to the extinction of the expectation that such behaviour will help to eliminate tensions or fulfil needs (Thorndike's law).

The result might be the circular aggressive process represented by the outer frame of Figure 3. The situation $S_1$ contains a series of cues for the secondary motivation $ES_{AA}$. The expectation of success ($ES_1$) leads to the choice of the aggressive action $R_{AA1}$ in the situation $S_1$. If that action is effective, then the secondary motivation receives further reinforcement and the use of the aggressive action $R_{AA1}$ receives its 'justification'.

If a person avoids sociable behaviour and finds that alternative behaviour fulfils his expectations, then such behaviour becomes reinforced. He is unlikely to wonder, let alone test, whether more sociable conduct might not have proved equally successful.

The assumption that such 'avoidance behaviour' is self-validating and hence applicable to quite different situations, is borne out by investigations in other fields.

Thus rats who have learned that they can avoid shocks by rotating a wheel, will continue to rotate the wheel up to 600 times, even though no further shocks await them (Miller 1948).

Once a circular process has become established, the expectation that it will produce successful results increases even further until, ultimately, other motivations fall into desuetude and the circular process may become compulsive.


## THE EFFECTS OF INCONSISTENT TRAINING

When we said earlier that aggressive behaviour has a high probability of success, we deliberately oversimplified the situation. The postulated expectation of success is a variable magnitude (in Figure 3 it was represented by the letter L [learning]); its intensity depends on the individual's 'learning history': in general, successes tend to increase it and failures to decrease it.

Let us illustrate this point with the help of our previous example:

John passes a fruit stall every day after school and, having eaten nothing since breakfast, he feels hungry. Force of circumstance, however, prevents him from satisfying his hunger by theft from the stall every day, either because another boy snatches the apple out of his hands, or because the stolen produce is rotten, etc.

Let his efforts be crowned by the following successes (S) and non-successes (N):


| Day | M | T | W | T | F | M | T | W | T | F | M | T | W | ... |
|-----|---|---|---|---|---|---|---|---|---|---|---|---|---|-----|
| Result | S | S | N | S | N | S | S | N | S | S | S | N | S | ... |


Here the expectation of success is not reinforced consistently but only in part or intermittently.

From a great many experiments (for instance, by James and Rotter 1958) we know that it takes longer to establish behaviour patterns through intermittent reinforcement, but that such patterns tend to persist longer once they have been adopted.

Let us try to apply this discovery to the learning of aggressive attitudes. Most teachers will tell you that they occasionally turn a blind eye to aggressive conduct. This means that the child succeeds with this form of behaviour and that his expectations of success with it are increased. If the teacher reproves the child 'consistently' between such oversights, than he engages in intermittent reinforcement. He will have helped to create an attitude that has become more resistant to extinction.

Parents often tend to expect their sons to behave 'like little gentlemen' at home, and 'like real boys' in the street, as witness the following interview (Bandura and Walters 1959):

FATHER: . . . One of those things that I just won't allow is for him to particularly get out of line with his mother or me, either one. Or if he were to try to use any abusive language or, you know, want to strike one or something like that, I just won't allow it.

BOY: . . . I'm not trying to be conceited or anything, but I know I can use my feet better than all the guys I hang around with . . . Like my Dad, he said, 'If you know how to fight with your feet, then it's in your hands, you've got it made . . . You never need be afraid of anybody.'

Conflicting, situation-specific norms, too, can thus produce intermittent reinforcement of aggressive behaviour.

It may be objected that the interviewing technique of Bandura and Walters did not allow a proper control of the conditions under which the investigation was conducted. The same objection cannot, however, be levelled at the following experiment by Cowan and Walters (1963), conducted under laboratory conditions:

Three groups, A, B and C, of ten normal eight- to thirteen-

70

year-olds each, were allowed to play with a large inflatable 'Bobo doll' which almost seemed to challenge them to aggressive acts. During the first two minutes of play the investigators remained totally passive; next they responded to eighteen successive aggressive actions. Children in Group A were rewarded with a marble for every aggressive act (continual reinforcement); those in Group B were given a marble for every third aggressive act; and those in Group C for every sixth aggressive act (intermittent reinforcement). After this phase, the children received no further rewards for aggressive behaviour no matter how long their game continued.

The results confirmed our earlier assumption. Although children in Group C received only three rewards, their aggressive behaviour lasted longer than that of the other two groups, and quite especially that of Group A. This suggests that inconsistent behaviour on the part of the teacher may encourage more aggressive behaviour for the express purpose of gaining a reward 'after all', since the pupil knows from experience that such rewards 'must' come his way sooner or later.

## THE APPLICATION OF 'LEARNED' EXPECTATIONS OF SUCCESS TO NEW SITUATIONS

We have been assuming that a specific situation contains a series of cues for specific aggressive acts, based on past experiences. It is, however, possible to observe more than one type of aggressive behaviour or aggression-instigating situation in man. How can we reconcile these facts with our model? When John comes to the fruit stall B, must he repeat all the learning steps that led him to $ES_{AB}$ with the fruit stall A? Or can he tackle the new situation, $S_2$, with the experiences he has accumulated in $S_1$?

This theory of learning attempts to solve such problems by reference to the concept of 'transfer of improvement'.

Learning successes can, according to Thorndike (1903), be transferred to other situations, provided the new situations and the old contain similar releasers of specific forms of conduct (quoted from Eyferth 1964). What expectations of success John has accumulated with the fruit stall A will thus contribute to the development of a similar form of behaviour *vis-à-vis* fruit stalls B, C or D, provided the latter resemble A in, say, their accessibility, location in the market, number of potential customers, etc.

Since A and B, A and C, B and C, A and D, etc., must always differ in some detail, $ES_{AB}$ must become extended with every situation in which it leads to successful conduct, including such situations ($n$) that bear little, if any, resemblance to the initial one. The releasers of $ES_{AB}$ become increasingly general and correspond to an increasing range of 'stimuli' ($S_1 \rightarrow n$). This process is known as the generalization of stimuli, and has been studied by Walters and Brown (1963), whose approach resembles that of Cowan and Walters mentioned earlier.

Walters and Brown divided their subjects into three groups: (a) children who were not rewarded at all (Control Group A); (b) children who were rewarded consistently (Group B); and (c) children who were rewarded every sixth time (intermittently, Group C), for aggressive behaviour towards a 'Bobo doll'. Immediately after this phase, the children were allowed to play together. Members of Group C distinguished themselves from the rest by showing a significant increase in physical violence, e.g. kicking, hitting, etc. They seemed to expect general success from the kind of behaviour that had earned them rewards during the first phase of the test. In other words, they had extended their $ES_{AB}$ from $S_1$ to $S_2$.

On the other hand, we know from everyday experience that one and the same situation can evoke a host of different aggressive responses. In the case of John, for instance, he might have taken the apple while walking past the stall and

72

looking in a different direction; he might have picked it up while pretending that he was examining it, etc. . . .

We have been assuming that different 'stimuli' ($S_1 \rightarrow n$) can release identical reactions. Let us now see whether different acts of aggression can promise equal success in mastering a particular situation, i.e. whether $ES_{AB}$ can be extended from the aggressive act by which it was constructed (learned) to a number ($n$) of qualitatively different aggressive acts (generalization of reactions).

Lovaas (1961) handed fourteen pre-school children two pieces of equipment, each operated by a lever. In one case, the lever caused a doll to strike another doll on the head with a stick; in the other case, the lever propelled a ball to the top of a cage. During the ensuing training session, half the children were reinforced for making the responses 'bad doll', 'dirty doll' and 'doll should be spanked', while the other half were reinforced for such non-aggressive verbal responses as 'good doll' and 'clean doll'. In the post-test free-play session with the original two pieces of equipment, it was then found that the children who had been reinforced for verbal aggression showed a significantly greater amount of *non-verbal* aggression than the children who had been reinforced for making non-aggressive verbal responses. In other words, reinforcement effects can spread from one class of aggressive response to another, depending on the situation and the personal characteristics of the subject.

Weak persons, for instance, will be less inclined to attack stronger persons physically but may readily resort to corporal punishment of their children.

Dinwiddie (1955; quoted in Berkowitz 1962) had his experimental subjects write down their reactions to a series of frustrating situations. Those who had described themselves as anxious in a preliminary questionnaire, were found to express indirect aggression more frequently than those who had not so described themselves.

A person learns to distinguish what forms of conduct

help to avoid punishment in what situations, and hence to maintain and consolidate his $ES_{AB}$ at a relatively high level. While the selection of behaviour patterns is thus governed by the maximization of the expectation of success, the precise interpretation of a given situation depends on its external characteristics, and, as Dinwiddie's investigation shows, on the personal traits of the subject.

This tendency to maximize the $ES_{AB}$ may lead to the differentiation of behaviour. In respect of individual conduct, what we have here is the generalization of $ES_{AB}$.

### REMARKS ON THE AGGRESSIVE INSTINCT

We have just discussed the case of John's learning, through 'generalization' of his $ES_{AB}$, to develop various techniques for raiding fruit stall A, and to apply the same techniques to fruit stalls B, C, etc. Earlier, we mentioned the intermittent reinforcement of success expectations and concluded that it increases the frequency of aggressive acts and resistance to the extinction of the $ES_{AB}$. All along, we have been assuming that John steals in order to satisfy his hunger.

We shall now look at the existence of aggressive behaviour patterns that have struck many investigators as being 'insatiable', and that have persuaded psychoanalytically inclined writers, among others, to postulate the existence of an 'aggressive instinct'.

> Is not what men do to themselves and to their fellow men sufficient testimony to the existence of an aggressive drive? . . . For it is a horrifying fact that so much destructivity and cruelty is not bestial, but specifically human . . . Can we explain man's love of destruction, pillage and murder[4] without postulating the existence of a special instinct? I do not think so. [Kuiper 1969]

What arguments can we muster against this view?

As early as 1937, Allport (1949, 1970) spoke of the 'functional autonomy of motives': though an activity is first of all the means of satisfying a need, it gradually becomes independent and serves as its own motive. Similar ideas can be found in Newcomb (1950), Sears, Maccoby and Levin (1967), Tolman (1959), Bergius (1960), Berkowitz (1962) and Oerter (1967). Let us apply them to our own example.

At first, John stole in order to still his hunger, and after a series of successes (positive reinforcements) he developed a particular $ES_{AB}$. As the latter became divorced from the original motive, it began to motivate itself, i.e. it no longer served to maximize the satisfaction of a specific need (SSN max). The new motive to be satisfied is the $ES_{AB}$ itself ($G_{ESAB}$):

John now steals to confirm his expectation of successful stealing (Figure 4).

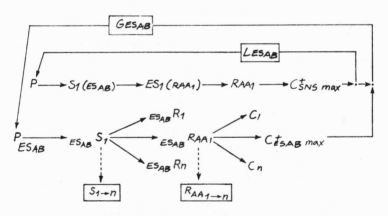

Fig 4  The functional autonomy of aggresive behaviour

Psychoanalysts maintain that the aggressive instinct is a constant source of aggressive excitation, and that it is discharged spontaneously. Allport (1970), however, pointed to a series of investigations in which the spontaneous activities of experimental animals could be explained equally well by his theory.

Thus Dodsen (1917) taught hungry rats to find their way through a maze. The rats subsequently crossed the maze even after they had been fed.

In human beings, we might quote the following example of a secondary motive:

To the infant the presence of his mother means first of all the satisfaction of his most elementary needs: the mother feeds, dries, warms him, etc. But after some time the infant resents being left alone even after the original need requiring the presence of the mother has been satisfied, and tries to attract her attention by screaming, crying, stamping, etc. Thus, while the presence of the mother originally served to satisfy specific primary needs, it has now become an end in itself (Newcomb 1950).

The authors we have cited thus suggest that the $ES_{AB}$ is a motive that, though based on another motive (e.g. the satisfaction of hunger, the thirst for power or possessions), has become the autonomous motor of self-confirmatory aggressive actions. It has become an end in itself – the person has learned to damage himself or others, simply in order to do damage.

In Figure 4 we have tried to represent this process as follows: once a person has learned that an aggressive act leads to success, he will see and possibly seek situations with this fact in mind ($ES_{AB}S_1$). He will similarly mobilize behaviour patterns for this situation by reference to the expectation of success ($ES_{AB}R_1 \rightarrow n$) and choose his actual behaviour on the basis of whether or not it can maximize this expectation ($C\ ^+_{ESAB}$ max).

### THE ELIMINATION OF AGGRESSIVE BEHAVIOUR BY THE DEMOLITION OF OLD, AND THE CONSTRUCTION OF NEW, EXPECTATIONS OF SUCCESS

From the preceding section it follows that we are unlikely to stop John from stealing goods by, say, allowing him to fire an airgun. What other means do we have to put an end to his aggressive conduct? Or, more precisely, how should parents and teachers deal with such 'symptoms' in everyday life? Do they really have to assume the kind of inner conflict postulated by depth psychology or look for regressive instinctual qualities?

Can we perhaps suggest the alternative of scientifically proven methods that are easily learned and convenient? The need to do so is all the more urgent since aggressive conduct is extremely widespread, as we can see, for instance, from the number of crimes committed in West Germany. Moreover, aggression also causes grave problems at school: according to Müller (1960) 41 per cent of the young teachers he interviewed complained of persistent disciplinary difficulties, as witness the following two replies to his questionnaire:

> Terrible disciplinary problems. Lessons often impossible because of the fighting and the noise [Questionnaire 172].
>
> It [lack of discipline] has affected me so badly that I have completely withdrawn from society [Questionnaire 191].

Teachers sometimes react to such infractions by employing the three principles of 'popular learning theory' (cf. Schwitzgebel 1964), which merely perpetuate what they set out to eradicate:

First principle ('repetition'): 'How many times do I have to tell you to stop stealing?'

Second principle ('punishment'): 'If you want a good hiding, just carry on thieving.'

Third principle ('moral lesson'): 'Can't you get it into your head that stealing is wrong?'

What all these methods have in common is that they place the symptom at the centre of the teacher's attention and that they are utterly counterproductive. The child is merely filled with fear of the physical results of his action and with inferiority feelings based on his failure to get rid of the 'symptom'. For the rest, he is never told *how* to improve, or what he should be doing 'instead'.

Thus Madsen *et al.* (1968a) tell us that when the teachers of an unruly class kept asking the pupils to sit down, they merely reinforced the symptom: the pupils ran about the classroom even more than before.

The problem can, however, be solved once it is granted that the social attitudes responsible for certain types of behaviour have to be learned. The human organism may be considered an information-elaborating system. So far, we have been assuming that people are capable of evaluating the consequences of their aggressive acts in a specific situation, either regularly or spasmodically. Now, whenever they master a fresh situation by aggressive acts, they are 'informed' (Foppa 1964) that their original expectations of success were correct.

Similarly, an aggressive attitude can be 'unlearned' if it does not produce the expected successes, in which case the previously established links between situation, expectation, action and positive effect are permanently broken ('time-out from positive reinforcement' – Ferster and Appel 1961).

In addition to decreasing the 'expectation of success through aggressive behaviour', and hence the frequency of aggressive acts, an effective method of re-education must also show how success can be attained by socially desirable means.

The modification of behaviour is therefore a twofold

process: the extinction of inappropriate behaviour must go hand in hand with the teaching of forms of conduct not only acceptable to the pupil's social group, but also deemed desirable by the pupil himself.

The teacher must accordingly ensure by observations or questions that the type of reinforcement he intends to employ enjoys a privileged place in the pupil's hierarchy of values (Ayllon and Azrin 1968). To that end, Staats, Finley, Minke and Wolf (1964) asked their subjects to select their favourite toys before the experiment; and Barrett (1962) asked her patients what music they liked best.

The modification of aggressive behaviour involves the construction of new success expectations through pro-social forms of behaviour. The subject is persuaded to 'relearn' things, i.e. to act differently in the familiar situation $S_1$.

In recent years, the method of extinguishing undesirable, and of reinforcing desirable, behaviour patterns has been used successfully to reduce aggression and other types of disturbed behaviour in all age groups.

Table 1, which is far from exhaustive, shows how long it took parents, teachers and clinical staff to modify undesirable behaviour patterns. Often they had the briefest preliminary training for their therapeutic task: their attention was simply drawn to the links between the 'patient's' aggressive 'symptom' and their own reaction to it. To that end the treatment was regularly preceded by a period of observation.

One of the first studies of such treatment based on operant conditioning was that of Williams (1959).

A twenty-one-month-old boy, who had been ill during the first eighteen months of his life, was in the habit of screaming and tossing himself about in his cot whenever his parents left his room, or even when they read a book instead of fussing round him. At bedtime, the parents therefore felt obliged to wait for thirty to ninety minutes until the boy was fast asleep. He had gained the upper hand because he could 'force' them to do what he wanted. To him there was an

Table 1. Examples of 'extinction of undesirable forms of behaviour' and of 'reinforcement of desirable forms of behaviour'.

| Author | Type of indiv. treated | Age (yrs) | No. | Place of treatment | Symptom | Therapist(s) | Duration of treatment |
|---|---|---|---|---|---|---|---|
| Williams (1959) | Boy | 1·9 | 1 | Parents' home | fits of rage | Parents | 10 days |
| Wolf, Risley and Mees (1964) | Boy | 3·6 | 1 | Clinic and parents' home | auto and hetero-aggr. | Parents and clinic staff | 180 days |
| Brown and Elliot (1965) | Boys | 3-4 | 27 | Kindergarten | phys. and verb. aggr. | Teachers | 14 days |
| Hawkins et al. (1966) | Boy | 4 | 1 | Parents' home | hetero-aggr. | Mother | 1 month |
| Sloane, Johnston and Bijou (1967) | Boy | 4 | 1 | Kindergarten | hetero-aggr. | Teacher | |
| Scott, Burton and Yarrow (1967) | Boy | 4 | 1 | Kindergarten | hetero-aggr. | Staff | 17 days |
| Ward and Baker (1968) | Girls + boys | 6 | 12 | School | DL* | Teachers | 5 weeks |
| Becker et al. (1967) | Girls + boys | 6-10 | 10 | School | DL | Teachers | 14 days |
| Bostow and Bailey (1969) | Boy | 7 | 1 | Clinic | violent aggr. | Clinic staff | 6 sessions |
| Thomas et al. (1968) | Girls + boys | 7-8 | 28 | School | DL | Teachers | 71 days |

| | Subject | Age | N | Setting | Behaviour | Agent | Duration |
|---|---|---|---|---|---|---|---|
| Broden et al. | Boys | 8 | 2 | School | DL | Teachers | 12 sessions |
| Carlson et al. | Girl | 8 | 1 | School | fits of rage | Teacher | 6 weeks |
| Madsen et al. (1968) | Boys | 8 | 2 | School | DL | Teachers | 16-20 sessions |
| Barrish et al. (1969) | Girls + boys | 10 | 24 | School | DL | Teachers | 22 sessions |
| Zimmerman and Zimmerman (1962) | Boy | 11 | 1 | Clinic | fits of rage | Teacher | Several weeks |
| Hall et al. (1968) | Girls + boys | 12 | 30 | School | DL | Teachers | 15 sessions |
| Tyler and Brown (1967) | Delinquent boys | 13-15 | 15 | Home | delinquency | Staff | 27 weeks |
| Burchard and Tyler (1968) | Delinquent boy | 13 | 1 | Home | auto + hetero-aggr. | Staff | 5 months |
| Meichenbaum et al. (1968) | Delinquent girls | 15 | 10 | Home | 'incorrigible' aggression | Teachers | 14 days |
| Brown and Tyler (1968) | Delinquent boy | 16 | 1 | Home | 'incorrigible' aggression | Staff | 3 months |
| Schwitzgebel and Kolb (1964) | Delinquent boys | 15-21 | 20 | Ambulatory | delinquency | Experimenter | 9-10 months |
| Bostow and Bailey (1969) | Woman | 58 | 1 | Clinic | verbal aggression | Staff | 5 sessions |

*DL – disruption of lessons

obvious connection between his screaming and his parents' presence and undivided attention. The parents, in turn, kept confirming his expectations.

The therapeutic directive to the parents was aimed at breaking this connection: after the boy was taken to bed at the usual time, the parents left the room and did not return when he started his habitual screaming. This method was rigorously followed lest the boy's expectations of success were reinforced intermittently. As it was, he stopped whimpering, stamping and screaming after the tenth bedtime, and now smiled whenever the parents left his room.

In other words, the symptom had disappeared without any threats or punishments. Nor was it necessary to blame the child's behaviour on neurotic mechanisms – the parents realized that it was their own behaviour which had helped to construct a time-consuming and completely pointless ritual.

In this example, all that was involved was the extinction of an annoying form of behaviour. From the reactions of seven-year-old Dennis (Bostow and Bailey 1969), we see, in addition, that it is possible to reinforce behaviour incompatible with aggression, and so to reduce the probability of the appearance of aggressive acts. Dennis was in the habit of attacking people and smashing furniture whenever he could. In the clinic and playground he had to be strictly segregated from all the other children. Sedatives did not decrease his antisocial behaviour. Next he was given treatment based on learning theory. During an observation period lasting for seventeen days, in which no drugs were administered, Dennis was allowed into the dayroom for thirty minutes at a time. During the subsequent therapeutic phase, in which he was again allowed to be with other children for a daily half-hour, a wooden box measuring 4 feet by 2 feet was placed in the room. The staff was asked to put Dennis into the box at once and without any comment whenever he showed aggression, and to let him out again two minutes later. If, however, during this interval, he had made no attempt to attack any child outside the box, he was given a sip of milk or a sweet, both of which he loved.

The result speaks for itself: while Dennis had originally committed some forty-five aggressive acts during each thirty-minute observation period, the number had dropped to zero after eleven days of 'treatment'. The time Dennis could spend in the dayroom was increased from three hours to the whole day within one week.

By showing verbally or non-verbally that the aggressive action has been effective, the victims themselves reinforce the aggressive behaviour of the attacker. Success depends on another's discomfiture, no matter whether he yields or submits (Patterson, Littman and Bricker 1967). In some studies it could be shown that a youth can attract the attention of his classmates much more effectively by antisocial behaviour than by socially acceptable behaviour (Baor and Harris 1963; Patterson and Ebner 1965; Patterson and Furniss 1966). This method of reinforcement can be avoided by the social isolation of delinquent children from others (Burchard and Tyler 1965; Tyler and Brown 1967; Brown and Tyler 1968).

Brown and Tyler report that sixteen-year-old John, who had been expelled from school as an 'incorrigible' case, and whose own parents found him intolerable, was made to spend the night by himself in a hut whenever he beat, threatened or bullied any inmates of the reform school to which he had been referred. This method was applied for three months, during which time the staff did not punish John in any other way, but went out of their way to express verbal approval of all his sociable actions. In later records, John was described as a 'model child'. The director reported at the end of the treatment that, whereas the staff had previously been unable to stop supervising John for any length of time lest he attack other children, John could now be allowed to go camping with the rest, and that he was on the best of terms with them.

The three children we have just mentioned were treated without any attempt to change the normal conditions of their lives by creating laboratory or other specially favourable conditions.

We have seen that reinforcement can assume various forms. Dennis, for instance, was reinforced by material rewards (sweets), John by verbal praise on the part of his teachers.

A show of appreciation by the teachers immediately after a desirable action has proved a very effective and easily applied method of reinforcement. Apart from certain exceptions (Wieczerkowski *et al.* 1969) we may take it that such non-verbal behaviour as a friendly nod, a smile, an encouraging glance, or such verbal behaviour as 'You did well','Perfectly correct', can be used at all times and in all places (cf. Allen; Hart; Buell; Harris and Wolf 1964; Johnston, Kelly, Harris and Wolf 1966; Holzkamp 1969).

Hoffman (1970), in a study suggested by the author of this paper, observed the behaviour of teachers in two classes of an elementary school and found, for instance, that 20 per cent and 18·2 per cent respectively of the teachers' general attitude to their pupils could be described as encouragement or praise. The pupils in each class had rated one another socio-metrically in respect of good looks, popularity, diligence and aggressivity. It turned out that those pupils of class A who were classified as aggressive received a significantly smaller number of positive encouragements from their teacher than did the non-aggressive pupils. Similarly, the teacher of class B encouraged 'unpopular' or 'lazy' pupils much less frequently than he did the rest. These results suggest that though teachers often make supporting and encouraging remarks, they tend to reinforce existing social structures and hierarchies. Thus the aggressive pupil receives far too few reinforcements for 'good' behaviour to develop new goals or new expectations of success.

This raises the question of how teachers can foster pro-social behaviour and attitudes by means of operant conditioning. In principle, pro-social and antisocial forms of conduct are governed by the same laws of learning. In his attempt to reinforce desirable forms of conduct, the teacher must begin by pitching his original demands relatively low. Thus Dennis was expected to act non-aggressively for only two minutes before he was informed by the present of a sweet that his behaviour met with the teacher's approval.

It is advisable to begin by reinforcing the desired behaviour continually, so that it increases in frequency. The highly aggressive, eight-year-old Diana, for instance, was given a 'star' for every half-day she spent at school without throwing a fit of temper. Whenever she had four stars in a row, she was offered sweets, and the whole class joined in the celebrations (Carlson, Arnold, Becker and Madsen 1968).

It must be the teacher's aim to build up the pupil's expectation that pro-social behaviour will gain him affection, attention or material advantages.

Once this expectation or 'hypothesis' (Bruner and Postman 1951) has grown strong enough to enable the child to draw freely on non-aggressive behaviour patterns, the teacher can pitch his demands higher and higher, and eventually resort to intermittent reinforcement.

The 'expectation of success through cooperative and peaceful behaviour' ($ES_{CB}$) is governed by precisely the same theoretical principles as we have adduced for the case of $ES_{AB}$. In Figure 3 the two terms are interchangeable.

## 5. Learning by imitation

### THE AVAILABILITY OF AGGRESSIVE BEHAVIOUR PATTERNS

The mass media play a much greater part in the teaching of aggressive behaviour and the resulting value judgements than is commonly realized.

85

'Cambodia is obscene – sex is not obscene!' With this cry, members of the Women's Liberation Movement and homosexuals broke up a congress of the American Psychiatric Society in May 1970 (*Süddeutsche Zeitung*, 15 June 1970).

It was also in 1970 that the Bavarian Supreme Court banned the import of pornographic literature even for individual use and not for resale.

By contrast, the law seems quite indifferent to the fact that between 1954 and 1961 the number of violent television programmes increased by 300 per cent (report by U.S. Government study group). The analysis of 183 entertainment programmes covering 122·5 hours of broadcasting time during a week in October 1967 and 1968 respectively showed that eight out of ten programmes involved acts of violence. During each hour of broadcasting, the viewers were shown fifteen violent scenes (Stiller 1970; cf. Selg, Ch. 1).

Or, consider the following findings:

(1) An analysis of the themes of fifty-one good-night stories transmitted to children by three German broadcasting stations showed that the category 'aggression and dominance' took first place among seven classes of motives (W.D.R.: 28·4 per cent; N.D.R.: 28·2 per cent; RB: 18·4 per cent). On average, every fourth action (24·1 per cent) was based on domination or the desire to dominate (Belschner and Schott 1970).

(2) A questionnaire sent out by the Schwabach Education Office showed that 336 out of 1,921 elementary-school children watched all six episodes of the extraordinarily violent television series *Tim Frazer*, and that they had done so with their parents' consent (Wetterling 1964).

It is questionable whether a moral code that (a) allows the killing of human beings, (b) has no objection to depicting the process of killing in every detail, and (c) offers acts of viol-

86

ence constantly and for no good reason as entertainment, is deserving of our support.

What can we expect of an approach that proscribes pictorial or written accounts of the sexual act as 'pornography', but sees nothing wrong with the constant portrayal of violence? Is it not likely that the frequent dissemination of aggressive scenes by the mass media will lead to a change in popular values and hence to the belief that conflicts are best settled by violent means? Is it really harmless to expose a large part of the population to the outpourings of television networks which Siegel and Gilula (quoted in Ilfeld 1969) have rightly called 'Schools for Violence'? In short, do viewers learn the technique of violence from their screen models?

### AGGRESSIVE MODELS AS TRANSMITTERS OF SUCCESS EXPECTATIONS AND BEHAVIOUR PATTERNS

During the past few years there has been a great deal of discussion as to whether such complex behaviour patterns as speaking, driving and also stealing, are 'learned' by operant conditioning. If they are, the various steps involved in their final construction ought to have been reinforced separately, when, in fact, (a) it is possible to watch the sudden emergence of 'ready-made' reactions in any one person; and (b) it seems unlikely that anyone could survive in the modern world if he had to acquire all his skills by operant conditioning, in which case the learning process needed for even the most basic skills would have to stretch into old age.

In 1941, Miller and Dollard investigated the process of imitation, i.e. the fact that 'one organism reacts to another by responding in precisely the same way as the other' (Asch, quoted in Haselhoff and Jorswieck 1970). They were able to show that the behaviour of a model M is only imitated by an observer O if there is a degree of emotional dependence between M and O, and if the successful imitation is likely to be rewarded.

Bandura and Walters, among others, have been trying, since about 1960, to explain imitative behaviour with the help of quite a different working hypothesis. In the case of aggression, the latter can be depicted as in Figure 5 and formulated as follows:

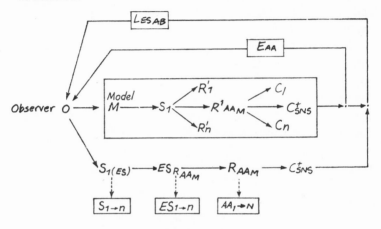

Fig 5  Learning by imitation

A model M employs the aggressive action $R'_{AA}$ in a situation $S_1$, and is observed doing so by O, whose behavioural repertoire does not yet include $R'_{AA}$. Careful observation alone is enough to help O adopt the 'complete' new attitude $R'_{AA}$ — O need neither copy the action immediately, nor need M be rewarded for his action. Months may elapse between the adoption (storing in the memory) and the first appearance of the action $R_{AA}$ in O (recall from O's memory store).

M can supply O, quite unintentionally, with a model for mastering a specific situation, even in the absence of a sympathetic bond or a teacher–pupil relationship. In other words, M need not be in the least concerned to teach O anything. Moreover, O's observation need not reflect a deliberate intention to treat M as a model or to copy him in any way. In fact, M and O need not even be acquainted with each other.

But in that case, why precisely did O adopt the new attitude $R_{AA}$?

Assume that John observes Fred, the class ringleader whom he dislikes, in the act of stealing an apple from a fruit stall and getting away with it. This observation can affect John in two ways:

First, it may help to enrich his behavioural repertoire with a new item ('ambling past the stall and snatching an apple while looking fixedly at the other side of the street'). John may store his new knowledge away for possible future use. (Here we shall refrain from offering a detailed account of this storing process. According to Bandura (1965, 1968) it produces a state of psychological excitation in the observer akin to that he would have felt had he himself behaved like the model. This state is said to be responsible for the observer's ability to recall the model's behaviour at will.)

Secondly, through Fred, his model, John has become acquainted with a new hypothesis ('if you are hungry, you can get food without having to pay for it'). The 'value' ($E_{AA}$) of the action for John is that he has come to realize that hunger can be satisfied in what, to him, is a completely new way ($C^+_{SNS}$). John has learned a new technique for fulfilling a need.

'Learning by imitation', therefore, means that the behaviour of the model stimulates the observer to imitation. The observer is handed a new instrument for dealing with a familiar situation, or shown how to use a familiar instrument in a new situation. In addition, his observation of the consequences of the model's action can lead to a reconstruction of old expectations. Thus O can, without ever having performed aggressive actions himself, develop 'expectations of success through aggressive behaviour' ($L_{ESAB}$) which may well affect his future behaviour in the situation S.

89

If O meets a successful, aggressive model at any time in his life, the result may be a new form of conduct – in which case we speak of the model effect in the strict sense; or the reinforcement of an existing attitude – in which case we speak of a 'disinhibition effect'. The stronger the hold of the $ES_{AB}$, the weaker the social inhibitions against aggressive behaviour in a given situation.

## THE EFFECT OF AGGRESSIVE 'LIFE-MODELS'

The model may appear in the flesh ('life model') or in 'symbolic' form ('film or cartoon mediated model'). We shall now try to establish whether or not these different presentations are equally effective in producing aggressive responses. Let us look at life models first.

Bandura and Huston (1961) offered two groups of pre-school-age children, A and B, a choice between two similar boxes. If the child chose the correct box he was rewarded with a coloured picture of an animal. A woman first demonstrated the correct procedure. In so doing, she used a number of quite irrelevant verbal and motor behaviour patterns; for instance, she would call out 'march, march' to Group A, do the goose-step, and furiously knock a doll off the box. With Group B, she approached the doll in a roundabout way and lifted it gently from the box. The children were then asked to play the 'game' in her presence.

Groups A and B showed a significant difference in the number of overt aggressive acts resembling those of the model: whereas 88 per cent of Group A copied the model's aggressive acts, 44 per cent the marching, and 28 per cent her verbal expressions, no children in Group B displayed such behaviour.

Quite generally, we may thus say that the model created a permissive atmosphere in which the child could not only learn novel forms of aggression but also perform them.

90

Moreover, life models are particularly prone to destroy inhibitions against aggressive behaviour.

A study by Bandura, Ross and Ross (1963) has shown that boys who watch an aggressive model display a greater number of aggressive acts against an inflated doll, including acts they had not learned from the model, than boys who watch a non-aggressive model.

All this suggests that what positive expectations children place in aggressive behaviour are reinforced by unchallenged aggressive acts on the part of the life model. The model is thus responsible not only for an increase in the number of aggressive acts, but also for the formation of new action patterns based on imitation.

All the studies we have mentioned were designed to determine the effects of aggressive models on individuals or groups under laboratory conditions. It is, however, possible to compare the aggressive behaviour of different societies. Thus it is clear that societies anxious to foster a military spirit will also tend to foster individual aggression. Textor (1967) has shown that there is a clear correlation between the importance thirty different societies attach to the idea of 'martial glory' and the incidence of individual crime. His conclusion is corroborated by the observations of other anthropologists who have spoken of the importance of cultural prototypes in the transmission of aggressive behaviour patterns from one individual to the next (Whiting 1941).

Parental attitudes, too, may affect the child's behaviour in the same way as a model does. McCord and McCord (1958) have shown that children are more prone to imitate the criminal actions of their fathers if the mothers, too, behave in socially objectionable ways, or if the children are shown no affection.

THE BOOMERANG EFFECTS OF PUNISHMENT

Many children receive corporal punishment at the hands

of their parents and/or teachers. Thus 55 per cent of all Bavarian boys and 37 per cent of all Bavarian girls have been beaten by their parents (Weber 1966). Hävernick (1964) has established that 80 per cent of German families approve of corporal punishment as an appropriate educational measure, from which he concluded somewhat rashly that parents who refuse to beat their children behave 'immorally'.

Until July 1970, teachers in Baden-Württemberg were entitled by a ministerial decree passed in 1953 to punish boys in Grades 3 to 9 for 'persistent malicious insubordination'.

Even renowned educators must be numbered among the upholders of such 'educational' measures:

In certain circumstances, corporal punishment is the only answer. Boys stand it far better than any other form of humiliation. A hiding is quickly over and quickly forgotten. [Hahn, quoted in Wolf 1964.]

Moreover, 44 per cent of the parents of German schoolboys believe that corporal punishment is a teacher's most effective means of controlling his class (Weber 1966).

Another questionnaire showed that although 66 per cent of West German adults put down love of children as their best quality, more than ninety West German children a year are known to die of 'child-battering' (unreported cases must account for a much larger number: Biermann 1969). In 1960, 235 adults were found guilty of this crime (Ullrich 1964).

Russell (1964) mentions a particularly striking example of how parents and teachers who resort to corporal punishment act as aggressive models: when he reproached a boy for bullying a smaller one, he was told that since this was precisely what adults did, it was perfectly fair. With these words, Russell added, the boy had summed up the history of the human species.

It is highly questionable whether beatings produce the

effect the teacher desires; what is far more likely is that the child feels hurt, disappointed and rejected. The result is bound to be a deterioration in his relationship with the teacher and vice versa (Tausch, Tausch, and Fittkau 1967). A positive emotional teacher–pupil relationship is, however, one of several important factors in lending the teacher 'importance' and hence in ensuring that his mere presence, let alone his affection and approval, act as reinforcers.

Learning theory takes the view that any teacher who metes out corporal punishment in order to eradicate undesirable aggressive conduct, behaves in a paradoxical manner: he prohibits aggression in others while using it himself as a legitimate sanction. The child receives a memorable lesson that aggressive behaviour is practicable despite everything the teacher has said, and also becomes acquainted with its effects (pain, etc.). But how is he to tell what positive actions are expected of him if all he is made to feel is that his past behaviour is reprehensible? Why should he change his system of values if his teachers adopt that system in practice?

Through punishment, moreover, his attention becomes focused on his wrong-doing, which may thus become reinforced. A study by Sears *et al.* (1953) shows that the more severely their mothers beat boys for aggressive behaviour, the more aggressive such boys become in nursery school – their models have taught them that force helps to resolve problems and conflicts.

Even when the beating is followed by the eradication of an undesirable form of conduct from a person's repertoire, it does not necessarily follow that the intensity of the associated attitude is reduced (see Chapter 4, pages 125-6). For when a person eschews aggressive behaviour because he is afraid, he may nevertheless retain his belief that such behaviour will prove successful, and this expectation can only be destroyed if aggression is consistently followed by failure (Alomon, Kamin and Wynne 1953; Ferster 1958; Bandura 1961). With beating, we may achieve no more

93

than a change in the locale of aggressive conduct: the expectation of success is shifted to social situations that cause less fear of such punishment. From the study by Sears *et al.*, for instance, we gathered that beating at home tends to increase the number of aggressive actions in the nursery school.

The boomerang effect of corporal punishment administered by the model (parent, teacher) can also be demonstrated by a comparison of the 'educational practices' of the parents of delinquent and non-delinquent boys (Table 2).

Table 2. Frequency of corporal punishment (Glueck and Glueck 1950).

| Corporal punishment | Delinquents | Non-delinquents |
|---|---|---|
| By the father | 67·8% | 34·7% |
| By the mother | 55·6% | 34·6% |

The less often parents offered their children a chance of observing aggressive models from close quarters, the smaller the likelihood of delinquency on the part of these children.

If may, however, be objected that the threat or use of corporal punishment is often unavoidable if an immediate end is to be put to some particularly objectionable act. In this situation the educator has to decide how 'severe' the punishment will have to be. That severe punishment is of little use in transmitting new values, i.e. in constructing new expectations of success or reinforcing old ones, can be seen from the two examples we have just quoted. The effect of the punishment may last while the teacher or parent is in the immediate vicinity, but it evaporates just as soon as he leaves the scene. Mischel and Grusec (1966) have even observed that the 'victims' may employ the aggressive behaviour of their model when the latter is still present.

By contrast, Aronson (1969) was able to show by a series of experiments that such mild punishments as a disapproving look may lead to the construction of new values by the child and not simply postpone the acting-out of undesirable behaviour for a short period of time (Aronson and Carlsmith 1963; Freedman 1965).

Let us take an example: John tends to beat his younger brother. If his father threatens him with a hiding, he will stop beating his brother while his father is watching. This external justification for his restrained behaviour is, however, missing if he is only given a mild punishment. John has to seek an 'inner' justification of his own by telling himself that there is really no fun in beating small children, etc. Such small beginnings may lead to the construction of a lasting system of values in which no success is expected from aggressive responses.

Several authors have pointed out that if the punishment follows the aggressive act after a long interval, as it so often does, then the victim may feel punished not so much for his 'crime' as for his attitude to the eliciting circumstances (Mowrer 1960; Walters and Demkov 1963). Thus if John is gloating over his successful theft at the beginning of the punishment, he may simply learn to avoid this particular type of emotional response. If a teacher makes frequent use of corporal punishment, he must expect to find that his pupils become steeled to the unpleasant consequences of their actions rather than renounce them.

Miller (1960) allowed his rats to find their way to some food at the other end of a maze. As soon as they started eating, they were given an electric shock, and the shocks were made more intense with every fresh attempt. In contrast to these 'experienced' animals, untrained rats stopped eating the moment they received the shock of maximum intensity. The first group had learned that the fear-releasing stimulus was a cue to the presence of food, so that they realized it was worth while continuing with the action they had started. This 'attitude' was applied by them even to situations in which different aversive techniques were used (Terris and Wechkin 1967; Terris and Barnes 1969; Terris and Rahhal 1969a). Repeated threats or physical punishments have much the same

effect on human beings: instead of persuading us that our behaviour is undesirable, they merely encourage us to persevere
(Terris and Rahhal 1969b).

We have been discussing several aspects of 'educational'
punishment. 'The clearest result of permissiveness in education during the past eighteen years is the increase in juvenile
delinquency . . . ' (quoted in Wolf 1964). But as we have tried
to show, there is no justification at all for the belief that
'tough' measures will have the opposite effect. 'We are only
just discovering the real meaning of morality. What matters
is how we behave to our fellow men, not how much of our
body we display' (Tynan, quoted in Leonhardt 1967).

## COPYING AGGRESSIVE ATTITUDES FROM THE MASS MEDIA

As we have pointed out at the beginning of this chapter,
the mass media are particularly wont to supply aggressive
behaviour patterns (see also Chapter 2). Here we must
distinguish between (a) film-mediated models; (b) cartoon-
mediated models; and (c) story-telling. We must agree with
Bandura, Ross and Ross (1963) that the tendency to copy the
model's behaviour will be the weaker the more unlike the
model is to a human being.

We can only mention a very few of the many studies into
the relative effects of the three methods of representation.
The effects of animated film cartoons have been investigated by Mussen and Rutherford (1961). A cartoon showing
aggressive plants or animals suffices to increase aggressiveness
in the youngest schoolchildren. In the interview following the
film cartoon, children who had seen a weed choke a flower
proved more inclined to burst a balloon than children who had
looked at non-aggressive and more cooperative plants and
animals. These findings have been corroborated by Lövaas
(1961b).

Larder (1962) played two stories to four-year-olds on a

tape-recorder. He set out to discover whether the contents of the aggressive (Group A) story or the non-aggressive (Group B) story had any influence on their ensuing play behaviour. He, too, discovered that aggressive contents encourage the use of aggressive actions in a permissive atmosphere: members of Group A preferred a toy in which a lever caused one doll to hit another on the head with a stick to one in which a lever released a ball.

The effect of films of a human model was investigated by Schönbach (1967), who showed adults a James Bond film and a Mary Poppins film, both preceded and followed by this question: 'Assume that you have been coshed and robbed and so severely injured that you have to spend four weeks in hospital. The criminal is of age and judged to be of sound mind. What punishment do you think he should be given?' The subjects were allowed to choose from among nine answers, ranging from six weeks' imprisonment to the death sentence. The number of persons choosing at least three years' hard labour increased from an original 28 per cent to 43 per cent under the influence of the James Bond film, while the tendency to aggressive reactions remained more or less stable under the influence of the Mary Poppins film (28 per cent and 27 per cent).

Eron (1963) asked parents to name the favourite television programmes of their nine-year-old sons, and then graded these films by their aggressive content. He next determined the children's overt aggressiveness by questioning their classmates, and discovered a clear correlation between the two sets of data. Eron's study does not, of course, tell us whether aggressive children watch aggressive programmes because they are aggressive to begin with, or whether their behaviour is based on that of their television models. It does, however, indicate once again that watching the aggressive behaviour of others does not reduce our own tendency to behave aggressively, i.e. that Feshbach's theory of catharsis (see Chapter 1, page 31) is untenable.

The studies we have mentioned so far were all conducted with a single type of model. Bandura, Ross and Ross (1963), by contrast, showed children, divided into three experimental groups, real-life, film and cartoon models respectively. A control group was shown no models of any kind.

Table 3. Frequency of aggressive reactions.

| Sample | Experimental groups | | | | | Control group |
|---|---|---|---|---|---|---|
| | Real-life model | | Film model | | Cartoon model | |
| | female | male | female | male | | |
| Whole group | 82·93 | | 91·50 | | 99·05 | 54·30 |
| girls | 65·8 | 57·3 | 87·0 | 79·5 | 80·9 | 36·4 |
| boys | 76·8 | 131·8 | 114·5 | 85·0 | 117·2 | 72·2 |

Table 3 shows how many times on average these children reacted aggressively during the entire observation period. While there are relatively minor differences between the overall responses of the three experimental groups, there are highly significant differences between them and the responses of the control group.

The individual reactions (not shown on Table 3) of which these totals are made up, show further that the greatest differences were between the control group and the two groups who had been shown film and cartoon-mediated models.

This does not bear out the assumption that real-life models provide the greatest stimuli for imitation. Moreover, the particularly strong influence of the film model refutes the view of Aubrey (quoted in Eron 1962) that there is no direct link between actions depicted on the television screen and the actions of children watching them. In this respect, it is obvious that what matters is not how much time children spend watching television but the content of the programmes they watch. As early as 1954, Hovland pointed out quite generally that the mass media – films, television, radio, popular books, magazines – might have a significant influence on the values and attitudes informing our actions. The assumption that an aggressive model tells the observer that aggressive forms of conduct are likely to succeed is convincingly supported by a host of studies published to date.

## CONDITIONS GOVERNING THE IMITATION OF AGGRESSIVE MODELS

These studies have also shown that the extent of imitation depends on a number of special factors. One of these is the observed result of the model's aggressive behaviour. Thus children who had watched aggressive models being rewarded with sweets, toys, etc., or verbal praise, went on to perform a significantly greater number of aggressive acts than children who had watched a model being punished for his or her aggressive behaviour (Hill 1960; Bandura, Ross and Ross 1964; Walters, Leat and Mezei 1963; Bandura 1965; Hicks 1965, 1968; Rosekrans and Hartrup 1967; Walters 1962, 1969; Walters *et al.* 1963; Thelen and Soltz 1969).

Considering them as substitutes for himself, the observer can learn from the behaviour of models and its consequences whether his expectation that a specific action will be crowned with success is justified in a specific situation. His willingness to imitate the model will be the greater the more convinced he is that such imitation will lead him safely to the desired end. Since it is merely the goal-attainment 'value' of such behaviour that counts in the imitation of the model's conduct, the observer may even imitate models he dislikes.

External characters such as great wealth, good looks, elegant dress and titles lend the aggressive model great prestige and persuade the observer that the model is in full control of his environment. This greatly encourages imitation, the more so as the observer assumes that he himself can use the same behaviour to achieve similar effects (Lefkowitz,

Blake and Mouton 1955; Bandura 1961; Bandura and Walters 1963; Walters, Leat and Mezei 1963; Epstein 1966; Soares and Soares 1969; Baron 1970; Baron and Kepner 1970).

Another factor worth mentioning is natural resemblance between observer and model (e.g. the fact that both are of the same sex and age) and the skill and status the observer attributes to the model (e.g. by considering him an expert in some field).

For reasons of space, we cannot here provide an exhaustive list of all the factors encouraging imitation. (For a further discussion, see Secord and Backmann 1964.)

### 6. Concluding remarks

'*Homo homini lupus;* who has the courage to dispute it in the face of all the evidence in his one life and in history?' (Freud 1930). The answer is: few, if any, under present cultural conditions. But are we not too hasty in attributing this sad state of affairs to 'human nature', the better to deny our own responsibility for it? Force is often described as the ultimate resort; but are we not much too quick to assume that we have exhausted all other possibilities before we resort to force?

In this chapter we have tried to argue that *aggressive behaviour is learned, not innate*. A wealth of empirical studies can be adduced in support of this hypothesis. Its most important consequence is that the reduction of individual aggression is not merely a personal, but also a social, problem. For our hypothesis forces us to ask:

1. What events in the individual's environment were responsible for incorporating aggressive actions in his behavioural repertoire?
2. What environmental factors have helped to maintain his aggressive behaviour?

These questions focus attention on the public responsibility for the origins and maintenance of aggressive attitudes. Cases in point are:

1. The failure to teach parents and others methods of non-aggressive education.
2. The constant display of aggressive models by the mass media.
3. The public acceptance of political strategies based on the threat of violence, and the admission of men with violent views to public office[5].
4. Public tolerance of war preparations on a gigantic scale and of war 'as the continuation of politics by other means' (Clausewitz 1832).
5. The fostering of an aggressive and tough masculine ideal.

This catalogue could be extended much further and suggests a host of social and political tasks, decisions and reforms.

From the assumption that aggressive behaviour has to be learned, it follows that the belief in the existence of an 'aggressive instinct' leads to acquiescence in aggressive behaviour as something perfectly natural, and can therefore cause greater social upheaval than aggressive behaviour as such.

Let us apply these ideas to the international stage. The belief that war is necessary, if 'only' as a last resort, is responsible for the arms race and the lack of resolve to settle all conflicts by negotiation. In that case war is, indeed, man's certain fate, and peace becomes an act of 'grace' or a 'gift' as it used to be in Antiquity or during the Renaissance (Nestle 1938; Raumer 1953).

*Homo homini lupus* – but only when he has learned to be.

**Notes**

1. Dedicated to my former patient Hans S., to whom I am indebted for many stimulating ideas.
2. This approach should be considered a counter-weight to the instinct hypothesis. We entertain no false hopes as to its implementation.
3. The normal distribution is one that fits the normal frequency curve. The latter is bell-shaped and symmetrical about the mean.
4. Here I must beg to differ from Kuiper: I do not love pillage, murder, etc.
5. During the summer of 1970, those attending a 'Peace research' seminar at the Teachers' Training College in Brunswick were handed a questionnaire that included the following questions. (The answers ranged from $1 =$ very great to $7 =$ very small. Because of the smallness of the sample ($N = 24$) the results must be treated with caution. The figures in brackets show the mean values of the answers.)

What contribution do the mass media make to the peaceful solution of conflicts? (5·29)
How likely it is that brutal films and television programmes will be banned during the next ten years? (6·00)
To what extent can modern Germans expect to learn how to solve conflicts (differences in opinion) satisfactorily from the politicians? (5·38)
How likely do you think it is that politicians will have exhausted every possible means of solving a conflict by peaceful means before the outbreak of a war? (5·71)

In short, these students did not consider politicians or mass media to be models or potential models of non-violent and non-aggressive behaviour. (Comparable results were obtained in 1971 from students ($N = 77$) and R. E. teachers ($N = 51$).)

KEY TO ABBREVIATIONS USED IN THIS CHAPTER

| | |
|---|---|
| $P$ | $=$ Person |
| $S_1 (S_n)$ | $=$ Situation |
| $R_1 (R_n)$ | $=$ Reaction, response |
| $R_{AA1}$ | $=$ Aggressive action |
| $C_1 (C_n)$ | $=$ Consequence |

| | | |
|---|---|---|
| $C^+$ | = | Positive consequence |
| SNS | = | Specific need satisfaction |
| $E_{AA}$ | = | Successful experience following an aggressive action |
| $ES_{AB}$ | = | Expectation of success from aggressive behaviour |
| $L_{ESAB}$ | = | Learning of $ES_{AB}$ |
| $S_1 (ES)$ | = | Situation 1 as releaser of success expectation |
| $ES_1 (R_{AA1})$ | = | Expectation of success from a specific aggressive action |
| $G_{ESAB}$ | = | Generalized $ES_{AB}$, not aimed at the satisfaction of a specific need |
| $P_{ESAB}$ | = | Person expecting success from aggressive behaviour |
| $C^+SNS$ max | = | Positive consequence of an action best suited to the satisfaction of a specific need |
| $C^+ES_{AB}$ | = | Positive consequence of an action best suited to confirming an $ES_{AB}$ |
| M | = | Model |
| $R'_{AAM}$ | = | Aggressive action shown by model |
| $R_{AAM}$ | = | Aggressive action copied by observer |

103

*Gottfried Lischke*

# 4. THE PSYCHOBIOLOGY OF AGGRESSION

# 4. THE PSYCHOBIOLOGY OF AGGRESSION

## 1. The psychophysiological correlates of aggressive behaviour

If we examine the linguistic compass of the word 'aggression' we discover that it includes, not only bad or harmful actions, but also certain somatic processes. We turn 'purple with rage', our 'blood boils', etc. Everyday language tends to assign an 'inner cause' to every type of overt behaviour. This alleged causal nexus keeps raising fresh hopes that the problem of antisocial aggression may one day be solved by physiological methods. People imagine the existence in the brain of something like an aggressive centre, the surgical removal of which would help to rehabilitate criminals; others believe that it is possible to develop drugs to inhibit offensive behaviour and hostility.

Such methods would, in fact, be much simpler and cheaper than laborious efforts to control destructive impulses through environmental changes. In particular, aggressive individuals would no longer have to be treated with elaborate systems of rewards designed to transform violent into cooperative behaviour. The possibility of purely 'somatic' solutions is also suggested by the belief that aggression is an instinctive faculty, a property of man's living substance, as it were. Hence,

107

what would be more natural than the attempt to deal with the somatic sources of aggression directly?

In this chapter we shall try to discover whether physiological methods of eliminating aggression have, in fact, proved successful or appropriate, or whether they have merely helped to constrict the individual's spontaneous and reactive behaviour to such an extent that his aggression, too, decreases in frequency and strength.

The connection between physiological processes and aggressive behaviour can be studied by two methods: (a) by recording the physical changes (e.g. in the blood pressure, the electrical activity of a given part of the brain, or the blood level of a certain hormone) accompanying (reactive or spontaneous) aggressive behaviour; and (b) by instigating or suppressing aggressive behaviour through direct physical intervention (e.g. electrical stimulation of the central nervous system, surgery or drugs).

Both methods aim at the correlation of experimentally induced 'physical' changes with the kind of behaviour that can be qualified as aggressive and quantified by psychological methods. Here we do not wish to enter into the problem of measuring techniques, for which the reader is referred to any good textbook of physiology.

## 2. Activity, activation, aggression, frustration and anger

Important and crucial in this connection is the definition of aggressive behaviour. In the studies we are about to discuss, aggression is not solely defined as the delivery of noxious stimuli but is also characterized by increased activity and/or signs of anger. Now anger, or rage, though not identical with aggression, is, in fact, the basis of the 'psychological' measurements used in most of the investigations we shall be discussing. For the sake of clarity we must first define exactly what we mean by 'activity', 'activation', 'aggression', 'frustration' and 'anger'.

*Activity* is the most general of these concepts. It may be considered the sum of all movements performed with the help of the striated musculature. It has a positive correlation with the sympathetic tone and the blood catecholamine (these terms will be discussed below) – though the correlation is not strict (see page 116, Schachter's experiments).

Activity is a prerequisite of aggressive behaviour, i.e. every aggressive act involves activity (cf. Bandura and Walters 1964). We do not, however, go as far as those psychoanalysts (e.g. Jackson 1958) who equate activity with aggression.

*Activation* is the physiological counterpart of 'activity'. According to Magoun (1958) and many others, the activation of an organism depends on the number of neural impulses from the ascending reticular activating system (ARAS). Morphologically, this system consists of a neural network running from the base of the brainstem to the midbrain. Its

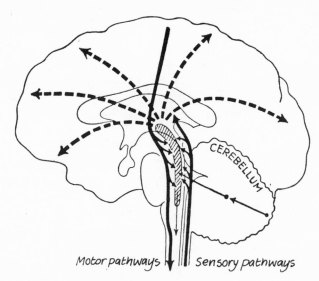

Fig 6  The ascending reticular activating system

anatomical boundaries are not sharp. The ARAS receives collaterals (side-branches of nerve axons) from nearly every sensory and effector pathway. After removal of this 'centre', all activity comes to a stop. Electrical stimulation of reticular structures in the midbrain can produce aggression in experimental animals. Similarly, the spontaneous activity of this centre increases with the blood catecholamine level. It would, however, be quite wrong to call the ARAS a 'centre of aggression', since its role in the general activity of the central nervous system is much too non-specific. On the other hand, a minimum of activation by it is a *sine qua non* of all aggression.

As for *frustration*, the term was introduced into psychology by Freud and developed by Dollard *et al.* (1939) (see page 10). For our purpose, it is important to bear in mind that, apart from pathological exceptions, frustration is generally followed by an increase in activity which, in extreme cases, may take the form of anger (frustration-drive hypothesis).

*Anger* goes hand in hand with an increase in sympathetic tone. It is often considered an intra-psychic correlate of aggressive behaviour, and since states of intense anger and intense fear are, by and large, accompanied by the same increase in overall physiological activation, it is difficult to distinguish them by purely physiological criteria.

By *aggression*, finally, we refer to all forms of conduct that damage other organisms.

### 3. Anger and fear

To determine the physiological correlates of aggressive behaviour, we can, for instance, allow our subjects to punish others by giving them electric shocks (cf. Buss 1961), or ask them to throw darts at distasteful objects, etc. In no case is there any guarantee that every individual will display aggression. Personal traits, group influences, etc., can produce

110

relatively strong differences in the intensity and type of reaction. After the provocation of anger and rage, it is possible to measure the physiological variables characteristic of these effects, and hence to take the first step towards solving the problem of the relationship between anger and overt aggression.

Physiological studies of aggression must distinguish the somatic state characteristic of anger from that characteristic of fear. Both states involve higher than normal degrees of activation. According to von Euler (quoted in Klopper 1964), aggressive animals, especially felines, have a higher noradrenaline content than non-aggressive species, such as the rabbit. Below we shall discuss the effects of adrenaline and noradrenaline in greater detail, but here we should merely like to point out that the adrenaline or noradrenaline levels affect certain psychophysiological values in significant ways.

Ax (1953), instead of trying to determine the adrenaline or noradrenaline levels directly, examined the physiological changes they produce. To that end, he created experimental conditions in which anger and fear could be produced in relatively 'pure' form. He used a polygraph to record seven characteristics (including pulse and blood pressure) in forty-three subjects, and obtained fourteen variables. The condition 'fear' was produced by giving the subjects harmless electric shocks while a laboratory assistant ran about nervously, muttering about a dangerous short in the high-tension cable. In addition, electrical discharges were produced near the subjects, who were told to keep absolutely still because of the danger, etc. During all these manipulations, the polygraph continued to record. To produce 'anger', a mechanic who was said to have been dismissed earlier, kept insulting the subject by reproving him for his alleged unpunctuality, telling him that his clumsiness had caused serious damage to the equipment, that his behaviour was stupid in the extreme, etc. Ax discovered that the subjects he tested for anger (the same individuals he had also tested for fear) showed, *inter alia*,

111

(a) a reduction of their normal pulse rate; (b) an increase in muscular tension; and (c) an increase in diastolic blood pressure.

No significant changes were observed in the temperature of face and hands or in the systolic blood pressure. 'Fear' caused (a) increases in muscle tension up to and including spasms; (b) increases in the electrical conductivity of the skin; and (c) rises in the respiratory rate.

Ax's findings suggest that anger is accompanied by increases in the adrenaline and noradrenaline levels; fear by an increase in the adrenaline level only. Though Schachter (1957) has cast some doubt on some of these results, Ax's experiments may be called classical in as much as he incited the state of anger systematically and recorded physiological responses to ongoing psychological experiences. However, Ax's method has one serious disadvantage: it is difficult to produce perfect records of physiological variables during such complicated interactions as movements involving the striated muscles. In this field, telemetry (the science of measuring a quantity and transmitting the results by radio signals to a distant station) has already opened up new horizons.

### 4. The physiology of ergotropic mechanisms

Ax's experiment (1953) clarified the relation between ergotropic mechanisms (Hess) and such effects as anger and fear. Before we enter further into the physiology of anger, we must first discuss several basic aspects of ergotropic reactions.

Cannon (1929), who did not refer to them as such, thought that ergotropic reactions helped to prepare an organism for 'flight or fight'. In the face of danger signals, the organism must brace itself for sustained violent activity, and Cannon listed the following physiological changes that occur when it does so (quoted in Buss, 1961):

(1) Slowing or stopping processes in the digestive tract.
(2) Shift of blood from the abdominal organs to skeletal muscles.
(3) More vigorous contraction of the heart.
(4) Deeper respiration.
(5) Dilatation of the bronchioles.
(6) Mobilization of sugar in the circulation.

These reactions are set in motion by discharges of the autonomic nervous system.

The autonomic nervous system consists of the sympathetic and parasympathetic systems. It controls the activities of the various glands and the smooth muscle and movements of the heart. This definition is functional. Morphologically, all autonomic nerves also contain sensory nerve fibres. This may be of importance to our discussion because sensory fibres are predominantly pain fibres, and it is precisely through pain that violent affective reactions can be triggered. The afferent and efferent parts of the system run side by side deep into the brain-stem. Even though the starting-points of the sympathetic fibres, with which we are mainly concerned here, are spinal nerve cells, they nevertheless receive impulses from the higher centres in the junction of cord and brain, in the midbrain and in the frontal and temporal lobes. This linkage may be considered the anatomical substrate mediating between the 'peripheral' and the 'central' physiology of aggressiveness. The nerves of the sympathetic chain constantly carry impulses that serve to maintain sympathetic tone. For anatomical and physiological reasons, the area under sympathetic influence tends to produce a marked spread of excitation; i.e. apart from local effects, excitation of the sympathetic part of the autonomic nervous system always leads to changes in the general sympathetic tone, the more so as the adrenal medulla,

113

the gland supplying secretions of adrenaline and noradrenaline, is served by a modified sympathetic ganglion (adrenaline and noradrenaline help to transmit stimuli in the sympathetic system). The perception of a danger signal, however, is followed by excitation not only of the sympathetic system but of the parasympathetic system as well. This was demonstrated by Rein and Schneider in the following experiment:

If a dog barks at a cat, the cat will show dilatation of the pupils, pilary erection, tachycardia, an increase in the blood pressure, etc.; in short, all the signs of increased sympathetic tone. If, however, the entire sympathetic chain is removed from the cat, then the same signal produces increased peristalsis, increased insulin secretion, and marked cardiac inhibition to the point of cardiac arrest. The cat may be said to have lost consciousness through anger. This shows that the parasympathetic system is activated as well, but that its effects are veiled by the more pronounced effects of sympathetic activation.

We must not, however, adopt the rather naïve idea that aggression is a function of the sympathetic system. Thus when Bacq (quoted in Rein and Schneider 1960) allowed a sympathectomized dog to fight with its brother for a bone, he found that the first was no less vigorous than the second. Animals whose sympathetic nerve has been removed only prove inferior to their normal conspecifics when exposed to severe stress. Their adaptivity has suffered.

We have already mentioned that adrenaline and noradrenaline help to transmit stimuli in the sympathetic system. Here the proportions are roughly 80 to 90 per cent noradrenaline and 10 to 20 per cent adrenaline. These two catecholamines are chiefly produced in the adrenal medulla (50 to 70 per cent adrenaline and 30 to 50 per cent noradrenaline). Although very similar in chemical composition, the two catecholamines have distinct physiological effects. In particular, adrenaline, unlike noradrenaline, produces greater clarity of mind and faster reactions. Adrenaline secretion is

114

stepped up in response to fear (Ax, Schachter, Funkenstein); conversely, the injection of fairly large doses of adrenaline in certain situations produces severe anxiety. It is important to remember that catecholamines taken orally are destroyed in the liver and hence have no effect. Moreover, no matter how they are produced or introduced into the body, they are quickly neutralized or excreted in the urine. This very property ensures that they are particularly suitable transmitters of transitory psychological and physiological signals.

The adrenal medulla yields its hormones exclusively after excitation via the sympathetic fibres of the splanchnic nerve. The latter receives impulses from the hypothalamus and the medulla oblongata. The precise ratio of the two catecholamines depends on the nature of the stimulus. Adrenaline is produced during hypoglycaemia (reduction of the blood sugar level below the normal value), and, according to Rein and Schneider, also upon psychological stimulation.

While adrenaline production is thus controlled by the brain, it may, conversely, have a selective effect on certain areas of the latter. Aggression research must therefore be concerned not only with the effects of adrenaline injections but also with measurements of the adrenaline secretion during aggressive actions. Unfortunately it is not yet clear how adrenaline acts on the brain. It used to be thought that the effects of catecholamines on the central nervous system are due solely to the fact that they increase the cerebral blood flow, but Vogt (quoted in Klopper 1964) has found that the highest concentrations of noradrenaline and adrenaline occur in the reticular formation, which latter must be considered the central activating system.

Rothballer (quoted in Klopper 1964) has adduced evidence pointing to the existence of central adrenoceptive mechanisms in the hypothalamus, which contains relatively high concentrations of both noradrenaline and adrenaline. From Rothballer's experiments it became clear that the hypothalamus is probably more sensitive to adrenaline than it is to noradrenaline. This brings us back to the question of the psychological effects of the two catecholamines. The answer cannot be based on the physiological effects because there is no clear correlation between the two types of effect. Hence we shall have to revert to Ax's idea and examine what psychological variables may be held responsible for the secretion of the two hormones.

Elmadjian (quoted in Klopper 1964) has compared the adrenaline and noradrenaline excretion of ice-hockey players engaged in aggressive skirmishes with that of the goalkeeper waiting anxiously in the rear. (The terms 'aggressive' and 'anxious' are not observational variables but interpretations.) He found that active aggressive displays were related to increased excretion of noradrenaline, while the role of the goalkeeper was associated with increased adrenaline output. From another experiment, Elmadjian concluded that boxers produce more adrenaline in the tense waiting period before the fight and more noradrenaline immediately afterwards. However, these differences in adrenaline and noradrenaline output might simply have reflected the degree of active exertion, so that we cannot place too much reliance on them. Thus Schachter (1957) was unable to reproduce Ax's results except in part. Moreover when, as an additional variable, he tried to reproduce the vasomotor constriction effect of noradrenaline, by plunging his subjects' hands into ice water, he found that half of them showed an 'adrenaline-like' response while the other half reacted in a 'noradrenaline-like' manner. Most of his anxious subjects, by contrast, showed reactions of the 'adrenaline type'.

Unlike Ax or Schachter, Funkenstein et al. (1954) worked almost exclusively with male subjects. Nor did they define the independent variable, anxiety versus anger, operationally; instead they fitted their subjects – who were asked to take a difficult test and were then goaded by electric shocks and severe criticism – into the two categories 'rage' and 'anxiety' depending on their reactions. Funkenstein discovered that the state of 'rage' was chiefly accompanied by cardiovascular changes of the noradrenaline type.

Buss (1961) has drawn attention to the influence of the intensity of anger. He quotes an experiment by Schachter showing that high and low intensities of anger are associated with adrenaline-like effects, while moderate intensities are associated with noradrenaline-like effects. If we agree with Buss that 'in laboratory experiments like those of Ax and Schachter the intensity of fear is greater than the intensity of anger', then it is clear that we cannot be too careful when associating adrenaline and noradrenaline effects with these two states. According to Buss, the nasty technician of these experiments may well induce great anger, but its intensity is mild compared to the intensity of the fear that occurs when the subject learns that 5,000 volts are loose in a machine to which he is wired. Were it possible to enrage the subjects sufficiently, then the physiological reaction might resemble that of fear, i.e. be of the adrenaline type.

In many animal experiments, starting with those of Cannon, no physiological differences between fear and rage could be detected. When an organism is faced with extreme danger, all its responses are heightened to the maximum extent, probably thanks to adrenaline-stimulated mechanisms. If we assume that this is indeed what happens, then the following experiment by Cohen and Silverman (quoted in Buss 1961) proves of great importance. They used airmen as subjects and their procedures included stress tolerance tests in a centrifuge, harassment, and injections of mecholyl, an anxiety-producing drug.

In the centrifuge, the subjects were rotated until they blacked out. The dependent variable was the pressure of gravity ($g$) they could stand before they lost consciousness. Urine samples taken before and after the experiment showed that the higher the noradrenaline in the urine, the higher the pressure of gravity the subjects could withstand. (This was explained by the fact that noradrenaline increases the blood pressure.) The subjects were interviewed by a psychiatrist and rated for both aggression and anxiety. Cohen and Silverman found that those in whom aggression was rated higher than anxiety could withstand higher $g$ levels than those with the opposite rating.

The next step was to reduce anxiety and to increase anger; in either case the $g$ tolerance was found to increase. Anxious subjects had relatively high adrenaline and relatively low noradrenaline levels to begin with, but after experimentally induced anger, they showed a very slight increase and sometimes even a drop in noradrenaline, while aggressive subjects showed a significant increase.

From these and other findings by Cohen and Silverman we may conclude once again that, though there is some link between anger and noradrenaline secretion, the correlation between the two is still rather ambiguous.

### 5. The physiology of frustration

So far we have paid little attention to the relationship between anger and aggression. A number of modern authors have suggested that anger is often the result of frustration and that it can be reduced by overt aggression, thus following Dollard *et al.* (1939). Their experimental techniques are, however, such as to blur all finer distinctions, with the result that increases in general tension are treated as consequences of frustration. These increases are said to go hand in hand with a sense of irritation. The tension is generally determined by measurements of the systolic blood pressure, a simplification that is said to make sense because several experiments have suggested that there is a clear statistical correlation between the intensity of the predicted reactions and the systolic blood pressure.

In 1961, Hokanson, studying the links between frustration or anxiety and overt aggression, discovered a negative correlation between the intensity of the aggressive reaction to frustration and the increase in systolic blood pressure after aggression. This was in accordance with the assumption by Worchel (1957) that verbal aggression reduces frustration-induced tension. Worchel, for his part, still believed in the existence of an aggressive instinct, and measured the reduction of tension or activation by the results of something like an intelligence test.

In 1961, Hokanson and Shetler varied the experimental conditions by introducing frustrators of high and low status, and again tested the assumption that frustration-induced tension could be reduced by aggression.

As a result of the experimentally induced frustration, the systolic blood pressure of the entire experimental group increased significantly, whereas that of the 'non-irritated' control group remained fairly constant. One of the experimental groups was given the chance to punish the experimenter with electric shocks during an alleged learning experiment; the other group was not. It was found that the blood pressure of those angered by someone of low status (a psychology student) dropped to normal once they had delivered a shock to the frustrator, whereas the blood pressure of those who had not remained high. By contrast, both groups showed a comparable drop in blood pressure when the frustrator was someone of high status (a visiting professor). According to Berkowitz (1962) this was because the subjects had no wish to attack him, with the result that the frustration-aggression chain was interrupted.

In a second experiment, Hokanson and Burgess (1962) tried to determine the influence of different types of aggression more systematically. Their dependent variables were systolic blood pressure and pulse rate. Both were measured before and after frustration, and after each of the following reactions: (a) physical aggression (administering shocks in learning experiments); (b) verbal aggression (completing a questionnaire with a chance of making a fool of the

119

experimenter); (c) fantasy-aggression (the chance of telling a story in response to a picture card); (d) the control response in which no aggression was allowed. It appeared that the blood pressure and heart-rate of frustrated subjects decreased fairly quickly after (a) or (b), but not after (c) and (d).

In other words, the type of aggressive response plays a crucial role in reducing tension due to frustration. The experiments also showed that the strength of aggression has no influence on the reduction of frustration-based tension – all that matters is the chance to engage in overt aggression.

Because they introduce several variables and precise measuring techniques, these experiments seem to demonstrate conclusively that aggressive behaviour reduces sympathetic tension induced by frustration. But, in that case, what happens to the demonstrable activating effects of aggression itself? In fact, though none of the authors we have just cited here correlated physiological variables with ongoing acts of aggression, they apparently succeeded in clarifying the links between frustration, physiological activation and aggression so well that Berkowitz (1962) described them as essential contributions to the social psychology of aggression and incorporated them into his own theory.

However, in 1966 Holmes arrived at quite different conclusions: experimental subjects, who were *not* allowed to behave aggressively towards their frustrators, showed a reduction in physiological tension, but not those who were allowed to give vent to their aggression. The dependent variables were again systolic blood pressure and heart-rate.

In 1967, Taylor discovered that the electrical conductivity of the skin, which is also increased by adrenaline and may therefore be considered a measure of general activation, rises after frustration-induced aggression, but not after frustration as such. The differences between Taylor's results and Hokanson's were said to be due to situational factors, and also to sex differences.

The introduction of environmental variables, however,

merely serves to disguise the real problem, and shows that the experimental set-up is somewhat unsatisfactory. If we also consider that individual differences were reduced to mean values in these experiments, then we must begin to doubt the usefulness of physiological variables in the prediction of individual acts of aggression under frustrating or other circumstances.

In 1969, Baker and Schaie confirmed the assumptions of Hokanson *et al.* They also found that it makes no difference whether the aggressive response is produced by the frustrated subject himself or by a 'deputy'; physiological tension is reduced in either case. This experiment cast further doubt on the alleged connection between aggressive behaviour and physiological variables. Gambaro and Rabin (1969) added that it was only in the case of 'low' guilt that aggression leads to a reduction in physiological tension – 'guilty' subjects retain their high blood pressure to the end of the experiment.

Unfortunately, in none of these experiments were the physiological variables measured after the subjects had been told about the various experimental deceptions. Might their blood pressure not have dropped simply because they were under the impression that the tests were of scientific value, or risen sharply because they felt they had been engaged in very complicated but obviously trivial tests for several hours?

The subjects had been frustrated, for instance, by being told to count backward from 99 to 0 while the experimenter interrupted them several times to say: 'At the speed you are counting the whole thing is a waste of time; you are obviously not taking enough trouble.' When they had finished counting, they were told further that the results were so derisory that they could not possibly be used. However, even when they were made to feel intensely guilty by being told that they were to blame for the failure of the entire project, the attacks on them were kept within academic bounds. True, the subjects were first-term psychology students who had to participate in a series of experiments as part of their training,

121

and hence realized that their cooperation would be taken into consideration at the end of the term. They were undoubtedly frustrated, as witness the significant increase in their systolic blood pressure. But is there really no more than a quantitative difference between this type of frustration and that which, according to Dollard *et al.*, and to Berkowitz *et al.*, leads to physical assaults? If the concept of frustration is to be enlarged by physiological variables, then we must devise appropriate experimental methods to cope with this extension. In that case, however, we come up against the methodological difficulty of having to assume that socially conditioned frustrations may produce lasting physiological changes. This, in turn, poses a host of serious problems, particularly in respect of the physiological effects of the catecholamines, substances that are broken down within minutes. The only way round this difficulty would be to assume that changes in the central nervous system lead to prolonged increases in sympathetic tone. In this connection we can do no better than describe an experiment, the methodological basis of which is open to criticism but which nevertheless points the way to a physiological (social) psychology of the future.

Fine and Sweeney (1967) set out to discover whether the persistent frustrations to which the socially underprivileged are exposed might not affect their catecholamine level. To that end they analysed the urine of twenty-seven army recruits on three successive days. Subjects from lower social strata (determined by several examiners from the personal files) excreted significantly higher amounts of noradrenaline (compared to adrenaline) than did individuals from the middle classes. The authors explained this difference with the help of Ax's hypothesis (1953) that aggressive states, and especially anger consequent upon frustration, produce physiological states akin to those resulting from the administration of a mixture of adrenaline and noradrenaline, while other stress situations tend to give rise to increases in the adrenaline level (adrenaline, unlike noradrenaline, increases insight and increases the speed of reaction). Hence the expression 'blind with rage'. Fine and Sweeney concluded that class differences are responsible for differences in stress control during the socialization of children: while the middle classes encourage reflective behaviour and tend to suppress aggression, the lower classes reinforce anger and aggression in their children. These two 'life-styles' lead to different psychological adaptations, and psychological adaptations are said to be responsible for the differences in catecholamine secretion.

Let us emphasize once again that our understanding of the psychological correlates of the physiological states characterized by the excretion of adrenaline or noradrenaline is still much too scanty to guarantee the validity of such interpretations. Physiological aggression research will remain confined to its academic ivory tower so long as its exponents refuse to heed the advice of Buss (1961) and fail to extend their investigations to the study of ontogenetic and psychogenetic problems.

## 6. The effect of cognitive variables on physiological states

The experiments we have mentioned were all based on the fact that anger gives rise to increases in the catecholamine level, and vice versa. However, as Schachter et al. (1962, 1964) have shown, this simple relationship does not reflect the real state of affairs in human beings.

Thus Schachter and Singer (1962) injected their subjects with adrenaline but told them that they had, in fact, been injected with suproxin, a new vitamin affecting visual perception. The whole experiment was presented as a perception test.

The authors divided their subjects into seven groups and introduced seven conditions as independent variables. In four, euphoria was induced by the methods described below;

123

in the remaining three the subjects were made angry. The first group was told that the alleged suproxin behaved like adrenaline – their hands would tremble, their hearts would beat faster, etc. The second group was told that 'suproxin' had no side-effects whatsoever, i.e. they were given no explanation of the physiological changes they were about to experience. A third group was misled with the invention that various parts of their body would go numb and that they would also have other physical sensations quite unrelated to adrenaline. A fourth group was given placebo injections of physiological saline, and was told nothing at all. The remaining three groups – those who were made angry – were 'told about adrenaline' (Group 5); 'not told about adrenaline' (Group 6); and given a placebo injection (Group 7).

After the injection, the subjects were asked to wait for some twenty minutes in a special room, ostensibly until the drug took effect. Next they were asked to take several perception tests to disguise the real purpose of the experiment. To induce 'euphoria', one of their alleged number, who was in fact an assistant, started to play about, for instance by folding his own questionnaire into a dart and throwing it around the room, by improvising a game of baseball with scraps of paper, and so on. If the subject did not react but continued to fill in the questionnaire, the assistant would aim the paper dart at him, play with a hula-hoop, and try in every possible way to induce a 'good mood'.

To induce rage, the assistant would protest violently about the test, objecting vigorously to such findings as 'does not wash regularly', swearing at such questions as 'How many times a week do you have sexual intercourse?' and completely losing his temper at 'With how many men does your mother have extramarital relations?' In no case did the assistant know to which group the experimental subjects belonged. The dependent variables were carefully constructed scales (based on observations through a one-way mirror), the subjects' own reports of their reactions, and a

124

questionnaire on the physiological effects of the adrenaline. All the subjects were male psychology students. The results showed that one and the same type of physiological excitation can result in distinct forms of behaviour. The two groups who were informed about the effects of the adrenaline showed neither euphoria nor anger; they were far less affected by the assistant's antics than the placebo groups. Those groups, by contrast, who were 'not told about the effects of the adrenaline' and 'misinformed about the effects of the adrenaline', produced greater euphoria, rage and aggressivity than the corresponding placebo groups. The experiment made it clear that the crucial factor in producing aggression was not so much the adrenaline as the cognitive interpretation of its effects as a releaser of rage and anger.

### 7. Sex hormones and aggressiveness

So far we have been dealing with catecholamines as aggression-releasing hormones. However, it is also widely believed that aggressiveness depends on the testosterone level – after all, bulls have been subdued by castration for millennia. Countless experiments (see Tinbergen 1956; Lorenz 1966) show that testosterone is responsible for rival fights in many animal species. However, we have good reason to think that this correlation holds for only those types of aggression that are a fixed part of sex-determined behaviour. Thus when Karli (1958) castrated highly aggressive, mice-killing rats, he found no decrease in their murderous tendencies. Rats that do not show aggression spontaneously, do not kill conspecifics or mice even after receiving large doses of testosterone.

Edwards (1969), by contrast, came to the opposite conclusion. He discovered that castrated male and female mice grew less aggressive, but that this process could be reversed by the administration of testosterone. Next, he administered testosterone to young mice from the day of their birth, and eventually castrated them. He found that, even after withdrawal of the regular testosterone dose, these mice proved more aggressive than the controls, and concluded that the precocious saturation of their organism with this hormone encouraged the development of neural structures responsible for aggressive behaviour.

For the study of the same effects in humans, we have had to rely on chance clinical observations. Thus Langelüddecke (1959) claims that the castration of criminals leads to a drop in aggressiveness, but others, including Kermani (1969), have been unable to discover any correlation between aggressiveness and the testosterone level. The methodological difficulties here – as in other cases – are psychological rather than physiological. Thus a very large number of men were forcibly castrated in the Third Reich, but the follow-up studies threw little if any light on our problem because their treatment of aggressiveness lacked rigour.

## 8. Central nervous control of aggressiveness

We have been looking at the links between the autonomic nervous system and aggressiveness and anger. A further development is to treat the central nervous system as a centre of aggressiveness, and we shall now examine the validity of this approach. To that end we shall be considering the case of anger rather than of aggression because anger, a violent psychologic process by definition, is simpler to measure than aggression which, though also a violent form of behaviour (Bandura and Walters 1963), can assume a host of different forms. With few exceptions (e.g. Hokanson *et al.*) there are no reliable experimental studies of the relationship between anger and aggression, or between aggression and the physiological concomitants of anger.

The hypothalamus is considered to be the most important

control centre of the autonomic processes. It consists of a group of nuclei at the base of the brain in relation to the floor and walls of the third ventricle. It receives impulses from peripheral receptors via the collaterals of centripetal neurones running to the thalamus, and directly from numerous cortical areas, especially of the frontal lobe. The efferent discharge pathways through which the hypothalamus transmits its regulating effects are the descending fibres of the medial bundle of the forebrain, the mammillo-tegmental tract and the dorsal longitudinal fasciculus. All three pathways discharge into the descending reticular system by way of synapses in the midbrain tegmentum. In addition, the hypothalamus is intimately involved with pituitary output, and hence with the hormonal balance; and it also receives impulses from the limbic system via the amygdaloid nuclei (Figure 7).

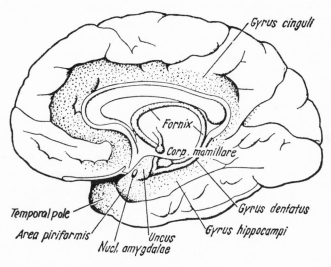

Fig 7 The limbic system

The limbic system is that area of the brain which constitutes the transition from the neocortex to the phylogenetically

127

older brain-stem. Its importance in the control of involuntary processes and the emotions was not recognized until it was found that lesions in this area lead to grave emotional disturbance. The limbic system consists of the limbic lobe (gyrus cinguli, isthmus, hippocampal gyrus and uncus) and the related subcortical nuclei, amygdala, septal nuclei, hypothalamus and anterior thalamic nuclei. Of these, the posterior area, i.e. the hippocampus and the gyrus cinguli, are believed to modulate the fronto-temporal area via the hypothalamus. After cingulotomy, animals become largely immune to pain and grow more 'courageous' in their fighting behaviour.

### METHODS

Ablation is by far the oldest method of studying central nervous control of aggressiveness. Cerebral structures held responsible for the inhibition or stimulation of aggression are excised or immobilized, and the animal's behaviour before and after the operation is investigated. It should, however, be remembered that the formation of scars, inaccurate incisions, etc., may have introduced significant artifacts.

Nor can the type of aggressive behaviour that occurs after, say, removal of the entire cerebrum, be truly compared with 'natural' aggression. A more accurate method is based on the destruction of precisely circumscribed cerebral areas by electrical means. Even more accurate results are obtained by electrical stimulation.

Thin electrodes, insulated except for their points, are introduced into the brain and a weak current is passed through them. After the experiment, the affected spot is coagulated with a high-frequency alternating current, the animal is killed and the spot examined by histological methods. The same electrodes can also be used to determine the spontaneous electrical potentials associated with aggressive behaviour.

In one particularly useful method, part of the brain is stimulated and the induced electrical activity of other parts is determined. This method enables us to investigate the joint activity of various cerebral centres.

More recently, chemical stimulation has come into favour. It involves the introduction of 'chemitrodes' into certain parts of the brain-stem. A chemitrode consists of an electrode and a minuscule cannula through which certain chemicals can be injected. When using electrical and chemical methods the experimenter must take care not to injure the efferent paths.

For a fuller physiological and histological discussion, the reader is referred to Hess (1954) and Holst (1960).

## THE MIDBRAIN

The ascending reticular activating system runs up into the midbrain. We have said earlier that a degree of activation is a *sine qua non* of aggression, and recent investigations have shown that aggressive acts can be induced directly by electrical stimulation of this area. Thus Sheard and Flynn (quoted in Kermani 1969) discovered that the central grey structures of the midbrain contain points capable of producing aggressive attitudes in various animals after electrostimulation, and that electrical destruction of these points leads to the permanent disappearance of such behaviour. The relatively non-specific action of midbrain structures may explain why injuries to the latter may cause the disappearance of aggressive reactions in cats (Sprague, Chambers and Stellar 1961).

Electrical stimulation of other midbrain points enabled Allikmets, Delgado and Richards (1968) to induce aggressive behaviour in monkeys. Injections of imipramine (a neuroleptic drug) markedly increased the threshold values of aggressive responses due to hypothalamic electrostimulation. Chlorprotrixene and promazine (two stronger neuroleptic drugs) proved even more effective. From the fact the Novo-caine had very little effect, we know that these responses were not the result of local anaesthesia.

Such experiments make it clear that midbrain structures play an essential role in the transmission of effects culminat-ing in aggression. Electrically induced 'hypothalamic rage' cannot, as it were, cross the threshold of the midbrain if the latter is blocked by drugs. According to Flynn (1967), the hypothalamus, by activating the midbrain, makes it receptive to releasers in other parts of the brain, and especially in the limbic cortex, and hence prepares the way for aggressive behaviour.

This activation has been investigated by Bergquist (1970), who was able to induce aggressive behaviour in an opossum by electrical stimulation of various points in its hypothala-mus. Next, he used electrostimulation to immobilize those parts of the hypothalamus from which neural pathways lead to other parts of the brain, and determined the respective increases in the threshold values of electrostimulated aggres-sive behaviour.

His complicated physiological and histological findings may be summarized as follows: in this primitive mammal the hypothalamus produces motivated behaviour by acting on the sensory and motor integration centres of the midbrain and brainstem. The neural pathways to the limbic system, to the thalamus and the cerebral cortex do not matter at this primitive stage of mammalian development.

## THE HYPOTHALAMUS

The hypothalamus is that part of the brain which, historic-ally, was the first to be associated with aggression. It played a central role in the Cannon–Bard theory. However, Cannon and Bard based their conclusions mainly on abla-tions. Thus Bard removed the entire cerebrum of a cat, and found that its hairs bristled, its pupils became dilated and that it began to spit and to scratch. This condition was described as 'pseudo-rage'. It was assumed that the hypothalamus would produce a permanent state of rage were it not inhibited by the forebrain. Pseudo-rage was found to stop the moment the hypothalamus was separated from the brain stem, and to be associated with intense adrenaline secretion. While experimentally induced rage could not, of course, be expected to resemble natural rage in every detail, it was nevertheless found to resemble it more closely than did those pseudo-emotional reflexes which can be produced in spinal-cord preparations.

The first to make a deeper study of hypothalamic rage was W. R. Hess (1954), who discovered that stimulation of certain hypothalamic points, often widely scattered, caused in cats hissing, growling, retraction of ears, piloerection and striking with the claws. That a real centre, and not merely an efferent pathway was involved, was shown by the fact that stimulation of a single point produced such very general and complex reactions. This type of behaviour differed from natural rage in that it could be superimposed on other forms of behaviour. Thus if the cat was stimulated while it was drinking its milk, it continued to lap even while showing all the reactions we have just described. Only when a suitable object for aggression was produced (for instance, the hand of the experimenter) did the cat attack. The rage reaction ceased as soon as the electrical stimulation was interrupted.

Hess's findings were corroborated and amplified by von Holst (1960), who investigated the responses of hens to hypothalamic stimulation. He showed that these birds would launch directed attacks, *inter alia*, on a stuffed weasel, but that it took a much greater degree of stimulation before they attacked such neutral objects as lumps of wood. Still higher voltages led to escape reactions. Von Holst stressed that the animal's mood has an important effect on the induced behaviour. He also studied the precise effects of repeated stimulation on adaptation.

Electrostimulation can tell us nothing about biochemical processes in the cerebral centres. A first attempt to investigate these was made by Smith *et al.* (1969), who introduced chemitrodes into various parts of the hypothalamus and then tried to regulate the mice-killing behaviour of laboratory rats with the help of various chemicals. They found that drugs resembling the acetylcholines caused peaceful rats to turn into killers of mice, and that acetylcholine inhibitors suppressed the killing behaviour of killer rats.

Every organism tries to satisfy its physiological needs. The starving want to eat, the exhausted to sleep, etc. If aggression, too, was an instinctual need, the organism would spontaneously look for means of meeting it. To put it more simply, aggression must satisfy. One early attempt to discover if it in fact does so was an experiment by Wasman and Flynn (1962). In this, fourteen of fifteen cats subjected to hypothalamic electrostimulation were found to launch directed attacks on rats, and these attacks resembled natural ones in every detail (see Leyhausen 1960). The attacks started immediately upon electrical stimulation and stopped as soon as such stimulation ceased. The cats greatly preferred living to dead rats. Some of the cats engaged in the 'affective attacks' described by Hess; others evinced the typical stalking behaviour of felines. A third group produced both types of aggressive response. Records of cerebral currents showed that other brain areas, including the amygdaloid nucleus, the midbrain, and the part of the hypothalamus opposite the stimulation point, remained tranquil. (Only in the hippocampus was it possible to measure increased EEG activity.) While Hess spoke of a defensive reaction, Wasman and Flynn thought that a spontaneous centre of aggression was involved. The cats had no external cause to show rage – they had not killed rats previously, the rats did not threaten them in any way, and they were not motivated by hunger since they did not eat the rats.

The results of this experiment might seem to point to the

existence of an aggressive instinct, and so might the finding of Lewinson and Flynn (1965) that the only objects to be attacked by the cats were their normal prey or enemies (cf. McDonnell and Flynn 1966).

On the other hand, Flynn (1967) found that 'hypothalamic rage' was purely aversive; i.e. that the animals found it unpleasant. Cats that had learned to avoid electric shocks by jumping on to a chair did likewise after electrical induction of hypothalamic rage. This indicates that the reaction might be due to some such thing as 'central frustration'. On the other hand, instinct theory would seem to be supported by the fact that the stalking behaviour was not aversive – the cats attacked stuffed or real rats, but no other objects. There was even a suggestion of a specific innate releaser of aggressive behaviour: cats deprived of their sight did not behave aggressively, unlike cats whose mouths had been desensitized.

Panksepp and Trowill (1969) also showed that the stimulation of aggression-releasing points in the hypothalamus causes aversive reactions. Using the experimental technique of Olds (1969) – a cage containing a lever that enabled the rats themselves to send a current into the stimulation points – they found that the animals could not be made to press the lever.

These rodents, which do not normally kill other animals, deliberately rounded on the experimental mice and bit through their necks. They never attacked dead mice or consumed their victims. The more distant the mouse was from the rat at the beginning of electrostimulation the more infrequently it was attacked. This significant fact showed that the victim was not actively pursued. Moreover, if the experiments were repeated several times, the killing stopped.

The authors consider these results prove clearly that electrostimulation makes the rats feel threatened until such time as they have learned that the mice pose no real threat to them.

The striking discovery by Abzianidze (1969; quoted in

133

*Psychol. Abstr.*) that 'hypothalamic rage' cannot be conditioned, may prove of great importance – not even by combining hundreds of electrostimuli with an acoustic signal was it possible to produce conditioned rage. However, stimulation of the same points with a slightly stronger current led to fear reactions that could easily be conditioned by acoustic signals.

## THE AMYGDALOID NUCLEUS

This area of the limbic system has a particularly controversial bearing on the control of aggressive behaviour. Wood (1958) has shown that bilateral lesions increase aggressive behaviour, whereas unilateral lesions do not; Schreiner and Klink (1956) discovered that amygdalectomy of various mammals leads to chronic hypersexuality, but not to aggressive behaviour. Galef (1970) found that rats were less aggressive but also less shy after amygdalectomy. Finch *et al.* (1968) were unable to discover significant differences in the aggressive behaviour of (a) amygdalectomized rats, (b) rats with cortical lesions and (c) normal rats. By a very carefully controlled series of experiments, Summers and Kaelber (1962) were able to show that of thirteen amygdalectomized cats, nine showed no changes in behaviour; two produced unclear responses; and two showed increased aggression. The two aggressive cats, however, proved far less enraged than cats which had been subjected to electrostimulation of the hypothalamus. Moreover, histological follow-ups showed that the amygdaloid nucleus of the two aggressive cats had not been completely removed. The authors suggest that in other rage-inducing experiments, too, the hypothalamic nuclei may have been injured rather than completely destroyed.

Let us therefore round off these conflicting results by looking at two sets of human experiments (Kermani 1969):

In the first, electrostimulation of the amygdaloid nuclei caused feelings of fear and anxiety. Once the two nuclei had been destroyed, patients subsided, lost their aggressivity and ceased to react to frightening stimuli. In the second experiment, twenty-four epileptics were amygdalectomized, whereupon most of them ceased to act violently.

These contradictory results may well reflect the fact that the amygdaloid nuclei have connections to most parts of the brain, so that wholly successful ablations produce different reactions from partly successful ablations. The nuclei cannot, therefore, be described as genuine 'aggression centres', even though electrostimulation often leads to states of rage.

Summarizing the results of forty-three studies of 'aggressiveness and the amygdalae', Goddard (1964) concluded that successful amygdalectomies eliminate aggressiveness in laboratory animals even if such aggressiveness was previously induced by septal lesions or by electrostimulation of the hypothalamus. Admittedly, anger can also be produced in amygdalectomized animals, but in their case the excitation threshold is much greater. Goddard attributes the differences in the behaviour of animals after amygdalectomy to surgical errors – the nuclei are minute and relatively inaccessible. It would therefore seem that the amygdaloid nuclei exert some control on motivated behaviour, helping to adapt the emotions to external pressures.

Pribram (1967) contends that the amygdaloid nuclei foster reward-gaining behaviour in conditioning processes. According to him, amygdalectomized monkeys show more violent reactions than normal monkeys and are easier to condition with fewer and smaller rewards. Andrews and Leaf (1969) think that this facilitation of learning behaviour is probably transmitted by noradrenaline, for rats whose amygdalae have been injected with that substance show a significant increase in such behaviour. Karli and Vergnes (1963) found that electrostimulation of the amygdaloid nuclei causes rats to behave more aggressively towards mice. These nuclei would therefore seem to open up other centres of aggressivity to motor activity.

The joint action of the amygdaloid nuclei and the hypothalamus was investigated by Egger and Flynn (1963) and Flynn (1967). They found that electrostimulation of both leads to increases, decreases or no changes in the interval between the beginning of the stimulation and the attack, depending solely on the position of the electrodes in the amygdaloid nuclei.

All these findings suggest that the more recently developed the brain structures in which the experimenters intervene, the more obscure and complex the results. Thus, though it was possible to define a few 'centres' in the hypothalamus, we are still unable to define such centres in the limbic cortex.

OTHER BRAIN STRUCTURES

It has also been possible to induce aggressive behaviour by stimulating other cerebral areas, e.g. certain thalamic nuclei of the cat (McDonnell and Flynn 1964), or by means of experimentally produced septal lesions in rats (Bunnell and Smith 1966; Wetzel *et al.* 1967). Delgado *et al.* (1967) could show that local injections of anaesthetics into the hippocampus of monkeys leads to a temporary decrease in aggressivity without changes in other behavioural variables.

SOCIO-PSYCHOLOGICAL REPERCUSSIONS

The fact that interventions into the central nervous system can lead to changes in aggressiveness and hence modify the social behaviour of animals was demonstrated by the classical experiment of Rovsold, Mirsky and Pribram (amygdalectomy of members of a band of monkeys, 1964). Bunnell (1966) arrived at much the same conclusion from his work with rats. A new method of changing social structures by direct intervention in the central nervous system was discovered by Delgado (1963), who studied four monkeys (*Macaca mullata*). Their 'boss', Ali, was very aggressive.

Delgado implanted electrodes into Ali's caudate nucleus, and then taught the rest of the band how to reduce his aggressiveness by pressing a button of a radio device. When the electrode was subsequently implanted in the thalamus, the radio signal served to increase Ali's aggressiveness. Both responses could also be conditioned to appear upon the sounding of a note.

As a result of this type of radio stimulation, the social structure of the band could be radically changed. The method promises to become a useful instrument in the study of aggressive interactions.

## 9. Genetic aspects of aggressiveness

Since this subject falls outside our immediate frame of reference, we shall merely refer the reader to the literature. A general account can be found in Fuller and Thompson (1960), and in Hall (1951). Kermani (1969) discusses chromosome aberration and its links with human aggression. (His results, however, are chiefly based on individual cases, and are moreover contradictory.) Popular opinion notwithstanding, it has not been possible to establish any clear connection between defective chromosome sets and aggressiveness. No additional Y-chromosome has been found regularly or in significant numbers in male criminals, and no one can tell how often this type of chromosome set occurs in the normal population.

## 10. Concluding remarks

The studies we have briefly reviewed may have produced many spectacular data, but it should be remembered that they have told us next to nothing about the genesis, predictability and variability of individual acts of aggression. The existence of a completely non-emotional, instrumental type of aggression may throw some doubt on the value of physiological studies in this sphere. It is true that we have learnt a great deal about the physiological mechanisms of rage, and we might well be able to reduce the aggression associated with such brain disorders as epilepsy by neurosurgical methods, but, in so doing, we come up against a dilemma that is also characteristic of other spheres of physiological psychology: we set out on a psychological study only to discover an increasing wealth of new facts with less and less bearing on our original quest. Physiological psychology is bound to grow in importance, but it will have to develop its own theories and methods if it is to make sense of its findings. As for physiological research into aggression, we must agree with Moyer (1969), that even in respect of internal impulses to aggression, the instinct hypothesis is a poor solution. And so we conclude with Vernon (1969) that aggression is too complex a phenomenon to be reduced to a single, unifying factor.

*Franz Schott*

# 5. WHAT IS AGGRESSION?

The definition and application of
psychological concepts

# 5. WHAT IS AGGRESSION?

## The definition and application of psychological concepts

### 1. Introduction

Because psychologists are far from agreed on the correct definition of aggression (cf. Selg 1968), we shall begin with an attempt to construct that concept step by step, and then go on to examine its scientific and everyday applications.

### 2. An attempt to construct the psychological concept of 'aggression'

With the help of ideas and experiences gathered in the course of research, it should be possible to establish whether or not our new construct of aggression is useful, whether it allows us, say, to describe everyday phenomena and whether it can be incorporated in a theory open to verification by standard psychological methods.

#### THE CONSTRUCTION OF A CONCEPT

Since everyday speech does not consistently assign the same meaning to the same words but reflects a host of prejudices, we cannot look to it for a precise definition of 'aggression' (cf. Roth 1963). Instead, we must try to develop that definition by gradual stages. (For the problem of the construction of a scientific language, see Kamlah and Lorenzen 1967.)

### A common occurrence

Imagine that A slaps B's face.

### The scientist's unconventional questions

A social scientist happens to pass by as A slaps B's face. Since he and the other two have the same cultural background, he immediately realizes what has been happening. Like everyone else, he knows that human beings often hurt one another, and he himself may well have delivered or received slaps. He might, moreover, side with A or with B, try to make peace between them, pay no further attention to the whole affair, or do more than one of these things. All this would be completely irrelevant to the progress of science if our observer – for whatever reason – did not ask himself psychological questions about the incident, and preferred to think about, say, methods of producing more effective slaps, or about what degree of physical pain the slap may have caused.

When we ask scientific questions about everyday problems (cf. Holzkamp 1968, p. 23 f.), we consider one among a host of possible fragments of life. This fragment can, moreover, be approached from various sides, e.g. from the viewpoint of physics, aesthetics, physiology or psychology. Again, if we adopt the psychological approach, we can ask a number of different questions.

Our distinction between the everyday world and the world of science is, of course, artificial, but it does its job if it brings home the partial nature of the scientific approach.

### Action and action schema

A historically unique event rarely concerns the psychologist *qua* empirical investigator. Thus the fact that A has slapped B's face just once is unlikely to arouse his interest. What he is far more concerned to discover is what the actions 'A slaps B', 'C slaps D', 'E slaps F', etc., have in common. In other words, he is concerned to argue from individual actions (cf. Kamlah and Lorenzen 1967, p. 94 f.) as to the action schema 'someone slaps somebody else'.

When a psychologist tries to explain to a colleague what he means by that action schema, he may adduce concrete or fictitious examples and continue to do so until there is a consensus. Things become more difficult if the colleague asks for a detailed analysis of the action schema. We shall now look at several aspects of such analyses and try to bring out their role in psychology. In the case of aggression, we shall see that these aspects have a crucial influence on its definition.

### The resolution of an action into 'behaviour' and its interpretation

This type of resolution is common in psychology. But is it necessary? Is it not artificial and dead? Does anything remain of an action if we refuse to interpret it? We must remember that two different forms of 'behaviour' may be interpreted in the same way. Thus A's slap and a curse may both be called 'hostile'. On the other hand, there may be different interpretations of one and the same type of 'behaviour'. Thus A's action may variously be said to be 'hostile' or 'educational'. For that reason it would seem useful to distinguish between behaviour and its interpretation.

*Behaviour:* By 'behaviour' we mean those activities of an organism that are 'observable', and hence open to objective description,[1] if possible with the help of physical measurements. Thus, in our example, we might imagine a three-dimensional coordinate system in which the movements of various points on the bodies of A and B are plotted against

143

the time, so that we can determine, say, the impact velocity of the hand against the cheek, once we know the mass of the head and the elasticity of the skin, etc. . . .

It is doubtful whether psychological research can benefit from this type of analysis. It may enable us to describe the action 'slapping someone's face' with the help of a graph, but it is most unlikely that even experts will be able to correlate the resulting curves with a particular form of behaviour.

The description of behaviour in the language of physics alone rarely proves useful in psychology.[2] The actions of individuals, with which psychology is concerned, are always actions that owe their significance to the (generally social) context in which they are performed. (A physical description of actions is, of course, an interpretation as well, though not necessarily based on the context.)

Behavioural psychology does not investigate every type of behaviour and not even behaviour as such. Rather does it study behaviour that can be described as action or part of an action. [Traxel 1968, p. 42.]

Now, when we try to describe, say, the action of slapping someone's face in the language of physics, it might be argued that, despite the objections we have just raised, we are, in fact, characterizing that action in a relatively interpretation-free way. Physical measurements seem to be free of subjective judgements. However, whenever we describe behaviour by means of physical measurements, we must remember that what we are doing is to translate a previously defined form of behaviour into the language of physics. Now, no translation can improve upon the content of the original; hence the description of psychological states in the language of psychology cannot be fully replaced by descriptions in another scientific language.

Take the following example: in a psychological test, the subjects were made to punish others with electric shocks of varying intensity (Milgram 1966). The actual voltage did not matter so much as the amount of pain the subject thought he was inflicting when he pressed the '100 Volt' switch. On this question, the subjects expressed the most various views.

Behaviour as the legitimate object of psychological research is any action that can be described in the language of psychology. Since the conceptual apparatus of psychology is not yet fully elaborated, we are still forced to employ everyday language in psychology to a far greater extent than in more highly elaborated sciences. Hence no psychologist should object to Wittgenstein's dictum that 'the confusion and barrenness of psychology is not to be explained by calling it a "young science" . . . For in psychology there are experimental methods and *conceptual confusion*' (Wittgenstein 1953, p. 232).

We asked what was meant by the 'interpretation' of behaviour. But what else is the delimitation and description of a given aspect or unit of behaviour if not an interpretation?

*The interpretation of behaviour:* In what follows we shall distinguish between three types of interpretation of increasing complexity:

1. By Interpretation I we shall refer to the attribution of a fixed meaning to a unit of behaviour considered in isolation. This approach creates special problems in the study of aggression (see below).
2. By Interpretation II we shall refer to the attribution of a fixed meaning to a unit of behaviour that has already been defined and that is considered in the (generally social) context into which we wish to fit it. This type of interpretation is used when we try to decide whether or not a given unit of behaviour is aggressive (see pages 151-2). In this connection, we should like to refer the reader to the important study by Levy (1963) in which the problem of interpretations in clinical psychology is discussed in detail.

3. By Interpretation III we shall refer to the attempt to fit experimental or everyday findings into an established theory. This is the most common meaning of the term 'interpretation'. Whether the theory provides a satisfactory link between the experimental findings and everyday life depends on how representative the experiments and relevant fragments of everyday life are to the theory. These problems will be discussed on pages 160-63.

Since various aspects of Interpretations II and III are dealt with in other sections, all we shall do here is to examine the case of Interpretation I.

When we isolate a unit of behaviour from the stream of events, it makes little difference which particular unit (action) we select and what we consider its essential features. We might, for example, pay greater attention to the exchange of words between A and B than to the slap. But if we are particularly interested in the slap, we must first establish what constitutes this form of behaviour – the slapping sound of the hand on the cheek, or the lifting of the arm and the victim's physical reaction, etc. Even in isolating certain behavioural units we are thus interpreting since, by using a particular approach, we attach special significance to particular actions, which we might not have done in different circumstances. In other words, we 'spotlight' a single point of an event, the size and colour of the spotlight depending partly on our intention and partly on incidental factors.

Once we have isolated a unit of behaviour, we must go on to give it a verbal definition for future reference. A videotape is no substitute for a verbal definition; we must also be told to what aspects we must pay special attention.

Here we meet a universal problem of psychological (and not only of psychological) research: no matter if a psychologist is planning new, or merely verifying old, experiments, he must generally rely on articles in the journals in which the particular form of behaviour with which he is concerned

146

is often described very summarily. Things are more difficult still when a psychologist not familiar with the field tries to pick up information from summaries or abstracts. Quite often the latter do no more than mention studies that support or refute a given theory and do not say how the results were obtained. The reader must trust the abstracter or else go to the trouble of obtaining and reading a vast number of individual papers and books.

The layman, finally, can obtain a totally false picture of aggression research if he reads popular scientific accounts in which the special conditions of the experiments are not mentioned or underplayed for journalistic effect.

Thus reading the report of research on a certain species of small mammal, he might easily have gained the impression that an 'aggressive substance' had been isolated and shown to be responsible for aggression (*Der Spiegel* 1970, No. 17). The real problems of psycho-physiological research into aggression are much more complex than the magazine suggested (cf. Chapter 4).

The danger of false generalization is particularly great in psychology because its vocabulary is studded with common-speech terms. Thus when an experiment shows that certain aggressive acts follow upon certain frustrations (cf. Chapter 1), we are not entitled to conclude that the same applies to all actions we commonly label as 'aggressive'.

But let us return to scientific practice. Here the isolation of certain units of behaviour described as 'aggressive' may lead to neglect of other important units.

Thus Lövaas (1961) refers as 'aggressive behaviour' to the operation of a lever that causes one doll to strike another. The title of his work is 'Effect of exposure to symbolic aggression on aggressive behaviour'.

The 'exposure to symbolic aggression' took the form of the showing of a film which was interrupted at frequent intervals. The experimental subjects (children) could, by pressing a lever similar in shape to the one which worked the doll, start the film up again. The object of the experiment was to discover whether children who had watched the aggressive film would operate the lever of the doll mechanism more frequently than they did another lever which simply propelled a ball to the top of a cage. The results were compared to the lever-operating responses of children who had previously watched a non-aggressive film.

Of the many types of behaviour that could be called 'aggressive', Lövaas chose just one, namely the operation of the doll-striking lever. In so doing, he ignored other forms of behaviour that might equally well have helped to elucidate the effects of symbolic aggression; for instance, whether or not watching violent films increases interhuman aggression.

An experimenter can only investigate a few, strictly defined, forms of aggressive behaviour. Moreover, the choice and successful experimental study of a particular type of behaviour often help to persuade a group of scientists to turn that type of behaviour into the chief object of their subsequent studies and hence exert a decisive influence on their discipline. This explains why the 'Bobo' doll (see Chapter 3, page 91) has played an important part in so many important studies of the learning of aggressive behaviour (cf. Bandura and Walters 1963; Bandura 1968).

When we look at an experiment we must take great care not to extend its legitimate sphere of application. It should, however, be remembered that in psychology it is impossible to do systematic research into more than a limited number of behavioural responses so that the psychologist must either run the risk of generalizing his experimental findings or else eschew all attempts to explain everyday actions. Still, he can try to minimize this risk by showing in what particular respects such generalizations are justified (see page 160f.).

The risk of generalization must be run by every scientist: physicists, for instance, have not yet established that copper in any shape conducts electricity in every single place on earth.

The selection of a unit of behaviour from the stream of events is thus an interpretation (of type I) with, as we have just seen, far-reaching consequences.

If we describe a particular form of behaviour as appropriate or useful, we are using an interpretation of type II. As we shall see below, it is often very difficult to make such judgements, or to decide what intentions underly a particular action.

*Can we grasp the intention of an action?* It seems obvious that a legitimate interpretation of an act must take into account the situation (and especially the social framework) in which the act occurs. Thus one's view of the slap may differ depending on whether A or B is a child or an adult, a man or a woman, etc.

Moreover, which perspective should we adopt – that of the actor, that of the victim, or that of the observer? (This problem has been discussed by several authors, including Kaufmann 1966; and Kahn and Kirk 1968). Since the action of slapping someone starts with A, the agent, we might try to discover how he himself views the situation and what his real intentions were. Did he merely wish to hurt B; did he have an ulterior motive, for instance to teach B better; or was the slap pure accident?

The intention underlying an action plays an essential role in the (type II) interpretation of that action. May a scientist, who, in his capacity of scientist, must strive for reliable results, attribute a certain intention to A's action? Might he not be deceived? This leads us to the hotly disputed question of what a scientific psychologist really can observe. Roughly speaking, the main protagonists in this dispute are behaviourists and non-behaviourists (an unhappy distinction that will, however, do for our present purpose).

Behaviourism is a school of psychology epistemologically related to empiricism and sensationalism, a school to which many psychologists adhere in theory rather than in practice.

Well-known behaviourists are Watson (1919), considered the founder of the school, Stevens (1939) and Skinner (1945). Critics of behaviourism include Strauss (1935), Smedslund (1955), Holzkamp (1964) and Traxel (1968). To the behavourist, scientific psychological observation is confined to such data as any normal person can discern. Interpretations (of type II), let alone emotional responses, are rejected because they cannot be the objects of reliable experiences and because they are not accessible to everyone. A's intention in slapping B cannot be determined irrefutably, whereas anyone could have seen A's hand moving towards B's cheek, and this apparently without the slightest need for interpretation. We have, however, argued that there is no such thing as an observation devoid of interpretation. Thus we should find it extremely difficult, if not impossible, to describe the visual object 'house' or the action schema 'slapping someone's face' if we refrained from all such interpretations as that the object in front of us is a house or that someone's face has actually been slapped. Moreover, we may well ask why, if the behaviourists are right, we do not constantly mistake our neighbours' intentions. Admittedly there are many misunderstandings, but, in general, we can rely on our interpretations even of social phenomena, and this precisely because they are not mere snapshots of our environment, but an active elaboration of impressions, characterized by the framing of hypotheses and their verification and correction (cf. Graumann 1956). Thus a psychologist, even though he knew little of the antecedents and the possible consequences of the slap, would be able to offer an interpretation that most of his colleagues will accept. In addition, he can interview A, and even determine whether or not A is trying to mislead him, and to what extent.

Psychology is nevertheless greatly dependent upon the good will of its experimental subjects. A behaviourist might stress the fact that there are constant misunderstandings in everyday life, but never in science, and that he confines himself to certain problems for the express purpose of achieving a high degree of observational accuracy. As an alternative to the behaviourist approach, we can, however, replace the assertion that a high degree of observational accuracy and scientific unanimity must be based on direct sense data and not on interpretations, with 'everything in the environment is observable and open to scientific elaboration provided there is a wide enough consensus'. If we adopt this approach, we are entitled to treat the expression of an intention as a form of verbal behaviour, thus remaining within the behaviourist fold. In fact, we rely on sense data whenever we ask what another person means, and the very fact that we are trying to discover what he means shows that we are not satisfied with his utterances, i.e. his isolated verbal acts.

We may be accused not only of vulgarizing the behaviourist approach but also of exaggerating it for the sole purpose of proving it wrong. But here we are not so much concerned with the various shades of behaviourism or the general importance of the behaviourist approach in contemporary psychology, as with some of the problems that arise during the behaviourist treatment of 'aggression'.

The question of whether or not we have to transcend the behaviourist standpoint is of great importance in aggression research, since the intention to attack (the aggressive intention) cannot be part of a purely behaviourist description. Unfortunately no generally acceptable definition of aggression with omission of intention has so far been adduced (see the critique of Buss's attempt (1961) in Berkowitz 1962).

## AGGRESSION AS A CLASS OF ACTION SCHEMATA

If we attach the predicate 'aggression' to the action schema 'slapping someone's face', do we mean that this action is morally reprehensible? If we do, we are appealing to ethics. Now, though both A and B may think that the slap was reprehensible, we may not be able to agree with them on purely ethical grounds. In other words, ethical considerations are no guarantee that we can tell, from the standpoint of the actors, whether or not aggression is involved in a given situation. Hence we are forced to adopt a relativizing approach, i.e. we must appeal to the ethical norms of the group to which both A and B belong. This is what behaviourists do when they define the delivery of noxious stimuli as 'aggression' (cf. Buss 1961). Now this is odd, for the noxiousness of a stimulus is not directly observable but depends on our judgement. But what precisely do we mean by 'noxious'? The answer surely depends on the prevailing group norms. It is, however, possible for an individual to be a member of several groups with different norms. Thus A and B might be members of a board of directors and also of a self-defence organization, and it might happen that B imagines he is engaged in a business discussion while A believes he is practising self-defence.

There is yet a third way of deciding whether an action is aggressive, this time without reference to group norms: by determining whether the agent (in our case A) intended to hurt B. In that case, we make the attribution of the predicate 'aggression' dependent on the agent's intention to harm or to hurt (to harm or to hurt in the sense that he himself understands these terms). Whether the agent's intention must be part and parcel of the definition of aggression has been discussed by many authors (including, particularly, Buss 1961; Bandura and Walters 1964; Merz 1965; and Selg 1968) and expressly affirmed by quite a few (Berkowitz 1962; Feshbach 1964; Kaufmann 1964; Merz 1965; Kahn and Kirk 1968). However, as we shall see below, if intention is taken into account it becomes exceedingly difficult to decide when an aggressive act has been committed.

We might propose the following preliminary definition: aggression is an action in which the agent intends to hurt or harm somebody (in the widest possible sense of the word). By looking for various action schemata that fall under this heading, we obtain a class of action schemata that can be quite generally designated as 'aggressive'. The following list is neither complete, nor do all the categories it contains invariably exclude one another. It is merely one way of dividing aggression as a class of action schemata into sub-classes of action schemata.

1. *Aggression for its own sake* v. *aggression as a means to an end.* Is the sole aim of the action to hurt the victim (aggression for its own sake), for instance to humiliate him, or is there an ulterior motive, e.g. to get at a toy or other object or to 'teach a child manners' ('instrumental' aggression)?
2. *Direct* v. *indirect aggression.* Is the victim attacked directly, for instance by blows and insults, or indirectly, for instance by depriving him of objects to which he is particularly attached?
3. *Means of aggression.* Is the act of aggression performed verbally, physically, gesturally, or with weapons?
4. *Real* v. *imaginary aggression.* Is the aggression real or imaginary (phantasied)?
5. *Self-* v. *other-directed aggression.* Does the agent direct his aggression at himself or at others? The problem of whether masochistic self-injury is a form of aggression presents special problems since such injury is intended to produce pleasure. A possible solution is that masochistic aggression is instrumental: a masochist hurts himself in order to obtain satisfaction.
6. *Planned* v. *spontaneous aggression.* Was the aggressive act planned or was it spontaneous (murder *v.* manslaughter)?
7. *Number of agents.* Is the aggressive act (e.g. war) committed by a few or by many? As with the 'educational' slap, or the slap in self-defence, we may ask whether a defensive war (e.g. to preserve 'Christian civilization', freedom, or communism) is an act of aggression. In much the same way as it seems impermissible to speak of collective guilt, so it

also seems unsatisfactory to assume a collective intention to injure. However, in so far as individuals kill, torture or malign others, or soldiers fire at others, for the sake of their country or in response to an order, they are undoubtedly committing aggressive acts.

8. Further elements in our catalogue might be based on whether or not a particular act of aggression is accompanied by hostility and/or anger. Buss (1961) has defined hostility as 'an implicit verbal response involving negative feelings (ill will) and negative evaluations of people and events'.

In this connection, we might mention just one more example of how difficult it is to grasp the aggressive intentions of others:

To avert a flood disaster, the population of a coastal region is forcibly evacuated. In other words, they are subjected to planned discomfort. Since the authorities expect that this operation will be welcomed by most rational men, and since they certainly intend no harm to anybody, we cannot speak of aggression – in contrast to what happened with the 'educational' slap, which was planned to hurt for pedagogical ends. But can we speak of an aggressive act if those about to be evacuated would rather stay behind? From the viewpoint of the potential evacuees, yes, because they feel that they are being subjected to planned chicanery. But the men responsible had no wish to annoy them deliberately: the sole aim of their action was to avert disaster.

It might therefore be better if we reformulated our preliminary definition as follows: the predicate 'aggression' can be attached to an action if, from the agent's point of view, its direct purpose (as distinct from the final object) is to cause damage or injury (in the widest possible sense). Thus, in the case of the 'educational' slap, the direct purpose of the slap was to hurt the child. In other words, it was an aggressive act.

But even this reformulation is far from perfect. It may

prove impossible to establish the agent's intention beyond reasonable doubt, especially when it is subordinated to, or associated with, other intentions. The conscious pursuit of a certain end can – depending on the nature of the action, the situation and the character of the persons involved – vary a great deal in intensity. It is exceedingly difficult to set a limit beyond which the alleged intention to hurt is strong enough to be called 'aggressive', and above all to verify whether or not that limit has been reached.

Again, if we grant that the aggressive intention does not have to be conscious, then we could easily call anyone an aggressor, simply by attributing to him undetectable, unconscious aggressive instincts. On the other hand, because people continuously hurt one another without realizing it – for instance, by air and water pollution, by socially approved forms of exploitation, by the uncritical repetition of false or distorted reports – any attempt to confine 'aggression' to deliberately hurtful acts may be said to exclude major causes of human conflict. But though we must undoubtedly pay serious heed to this objection, we must remember that even a definition of aggression based exclusively on the damage done is open to several objections. Perhaps psychologists trying to explain the behaviour and actions of individuals would be better advised to start with such personal features as aggressive intentions, rather than with collective assessments of the damage done.

Needless to say, a definition of aggression that involves the agent's intention can only apply to individuals whom we can question and not to infants who have not yet learned to verbalize their motives; in their case, and in that of animals, we can only speak of 'aggression-like' behaviour. Buss's definition (aggression is the delivery of noxious stimuli) has, on the other hand, the advantage that it enables us to attribute aggression to all living organisms, which is the more important in that many experiments in our field are made with animals and small children. It does, however, entail many difficulties and even dangers besides those we have already mentioned. We far too readily anthropomorphize the behaviour of animals and fit young children into adult categories. If we do that, we may begin to marvel, say, at the light which animal behaviour apparently throws on human actions until we notice that we have been caught in a vicious circle: the human stereotypes we originally applied to animals prove, not surprisingly, to fit human behaviour most perfectly. (As an illustration, the reader is referred to Lorenz (1966) and his critics, Barnett (1967) and Rattner (1970).) Whether we can apply the experimental findings made with one species of animal to another or to man depends on our prior estimate of their similarities.

Selg has extended Buss's definition as follows: 'Aggression is the delivery of noxious stimuli to an organism or to a substitute . . . ' (Selg 1968, p. 22). In other words, Selg proposes to define aggression, not by the agent's intention, but by his observable actions. But, as we saw, it is highly problematic whether an external observer can interpret human actions without considering the underlying intentions.

'How nice of you to have tidied my desk!' a listener may hear a husband say to his wife. Is he being sarcastic? And if the wife fails to reply, is she trying to add insult to injury?

In particular, if we take the view that all scientific actions are guided by theories (e.g. Holzkamp 1968), we cannot advance a definition of aggression based on psychological experiments involving statistical manipulations without adequate theoretical reflection. Empirical conclusions obtained without a theoretical framework can be interpreted in any number of ways and are therefore quite meaningless. Nor can we decide on the correctness of a definition by a show of hands – and this quite apart from the fact that definitions, like theories, are neither true nor false but more or less useful. It is only fair, however, to point out that authors close to neopositivism (often called logical empiricism; cf. Kraft 1950; Stegmüller 1965) contend that all research is guided by experience and that it is possible to design theory-free experiments when opening up new scientific territory.

In my view, every form of research must bear on a theoretical framework that does not, however, have to be its antecedent in time. It may, for instance, become clear after the event that certain experimental results presuppose a certain approach or theory, however rudimentary. For the critical evaluation of a research project, it is essential, *inter alia*, to look at what attitudes and views have guided a group of research workers but which have not been, and indeed could not have been, incorporated in their final report (cf. Kuhn 1967). Thus, partly for historico-psychological reasons, much of contemporary research into aggression seems to be guided by social learning theory, and many experiments have been designed accordingly. This may explain the type, frequency and tendency of modern research, but does not help us to assess the importance of individual discoveries.

As with many definitions, we have to decide how wide we wish to make our concept of 'aggression'. Too narrow a definition (e.g. one that discards instrumental aggression from the outset) may encourage a host of impermissible generalizations, i.e. tempt us to ignore what conceptual limitations we ourselves have introduced. Awareness of these limitations helps us to see problems more sharply and to ask more relevant questions. Again, too broad a definition (e.g. Kelly's definition that every active structuring of the perceptive field must be considered a form of aggression; cf. Wepman and Heine 1963) may lend itself to a host of completely meaningless applications.

We can sum up by saying that none of the definitions of aggression we have mentioned can be called satisfactory in all respects, and that there cannot, in fact, be a fully satisfactory definition while we continue to borrow the vague and equivocal word 'aggression' from common speech. Common usage may suggest the possible scope of a definition, but science alone can give it adequate sharpness. For the evaluation of particular results in aggression research, it is therefore essential to bear in mind on what original definition of aggression they have been based, and this all the more so if we wish to apply the results to problems of daily life.

## AGGRESSIVENESS AS A PSYCHOLOGICAL PREDISPOSITION TO AGGRESSION

If an individual performs several actions that fall into a certain class of action schemata, we tend to attach certain qualities to him. In the case of aggressive actions, for instance, we speak of his aggressiveness or psychological predisposition to aggression. Depending on our theoretical approach, we call this quality a drive, instinct, motive, capacity, tendency or hypothetical construct (cf. Graumann 1960; Roth 1963; Roth 1969). The last of these terms has become highly fashionable (for 'construct', see Cronbach and Meehl 1955; Hörmann 1964; Herrmann 1969; Schneewind 1969), and is being used more or less as a synonym for 'research concept'. Those employing it are rightly determined to banish the search for man's 'true essence' from psychology (e.g. Herrmann 1969), but, understandably enough, they are not prepared to accept a totally atheoretical correlation of directly observable behaviour data (e.g. Cronbach and Meehl 1955). Most writers apply the term 'construct' not to a directly observable, but rather to a theoretical, construction that may become more precise with the progress of science, but can never be complete. This kind of theoretical construction is said to play a useful part in the description or explanation of empirical states of affair.

At what point we cease speaking of observables and introduce the idea of constructs depends on what we consider perceptible (cf. Seiffert 1969). A behaviourist, for example, would include aggression, as we have tried to define it (in so far as he agrees with this definition at all), among the constructs; indeed, most psychologists would treat 'aggressiveness' in that way. Others, however, often because they are determined to use concrete examples, mistakenly reify 'constructs' and turn them into material entities (cf. Holzkamp 1964; Selg 1966).

To make this point clear, we need merely ask whether there is such a thing as 'aggressiveness'. 'Of course there is,' we shall be told, 'you have only to look around.' But then we may go on to ask if there is such a thing as 'well-I-never-ness', i.e. the psychological predisposition to say 'Well, I never!' Clearly, we could demonstrate the existence of this particular quality. We can always call the tendency to behave in a certain way a psychological predisposition. Therefore we proceed quite arbitrarily when we isolate certain behavioural units, call them aggressive acts, and attribute to them the psychological predisposition called 'aggressiveness'. What happens more generally, however, is that common speech and usage persuade psychologists to construct certain research units. This was no doubt the origin of research into aggression. However, psychology which, *inter alia*, tries to construct theories about the behaviour of organisms is left with the question of whether or not it is useful to attach a psychological predisposition to many classes of action schema (as was done, for instance, in the compilation of the list of so-called instincts; cf. McDougall 1947). This procedure can earn psychology nothing but new words, and in order to avoid this useless accumulation of concepts, we should refrain, for instance, from incorporating 'aggressiveness' into our technical vocabulary unless there are weighty reasons for doing so (e.g. the historical significance of this concept, or the large number of contributions to modern research that could be classified under that heading). For the rest, it would probably be more economical to try to explain the occurrence of aggression with the help of such established concepts as intelligence and motor activity. Thus Patterson *et al.* (1967) consider aggressive behaviour a sub-class of 'assertive behaviour'.

159

### 3. The application of psychological concepts to research

Having looked at various ways of defining aggression, we shall now turn our attention to some of the problems that may arise when we try to apply a psychological concept (such as aggression) to practical research. We shall choose two examples.

#### OPERATIONAL DEFINITIONS

The better to guard against unclear definitions, 'operationists'[3] demand that every concept be defined by the operations that help to construct it and, generally, to measure it as well. Thus 'aggressiveness' would be what can be measured by the aggressiveness-test XYZ. Strictly speaking, an operational definition is no definition at all but a set of experimental directives to realize something defined beforehand. If that were not so, we might call any test whatsoever an aggressiveness test. But, in that case, we should have to justify our doing so on demand, and the only justification we or anyone else could offer would be one involving an extant theoretical concept. In other words, it is not enough to provide an operational 'definition' of aggression or aggressiveness.

#### THE PROBLEM OF REPRESENTATION

What do we do when we verify a particular theory by experimental methods (cf. Holzkamp 1964)? Take the intentional definition of aggression, and assume, in accordance with a certain theory, that man learns his aggressiveness from models whose aggressive acts have proved successful. We could then devise the following experimental test of our assumption:

We divide a group of pre-school children into two random groups, and show to one a 'supermouse' film. Thanks to his 'supermousy' powers, the hero of this film easily keeps the evil cat at bay. The other group of children is shown a film of Mickey Mouse travelling peacefully in a strange vehicle through the Land of Contented Cows. After the films have been shown, both groups of children return to their usual games. Aggressive actions during the next hour are watched and counted in order to determine which, if any, group commits the larger number of such acts.

Now, regardless of the results, we must ask ourselves whether and to what extent this experiment is, in fact, capable of verifying our theory. If we fail to do so, we run the risk of considering as significant none but experiments that bear out our original hypothesis. We must therefore make sure that the set-up and properties are such as to provide a real test of our theoretical assumptions, i.e. we must investigate whether our experimental statements (i.e. our technical directives to the experimenter) are 'representative' of our theoretical statements (cf. Holzkamp 1964). To do that we must have suitable criteria, as we shall now try to make clear (incompletely) with the help of our film experiment.

(a) *Environmental aspects:* Our theory does not call for a special environment, which suggests that the environmental element plays no part in it. In other words, the same effect could be obtained in every culture, provided only that the correct experimental set-up is used.

(b) *Humans and animals:* Since the two films were obviously designed for humans, we cannot simply apply the results of the experiment to the animal kingdom at large. Conversely, we cannot apply the results of animal experiments to human aggressiveness.

(c) *Duration.* Since our theory does not confine the learning of aggression to any particular stage of development, we may assume either that aggression is learned throughout human life or that the time factor is irrelevant. We must therefore

161

ask if a single showing of the film is 'representative' of this assumption. In addition, we must ask whether the interval between the showing of the film and the observation of the aggressive act and also the time devoted to this observation are representative of the duration of adult life.

In their fascinating study, Dollard *et al.* (1939) tried to explain the rise of German Fascism by the frustration-aggression hypothesis (see Chapter 1). But while the political process took many years, the F-A experiments devoted to it took a few hours at most. Hence these experiments cannot throw much light on the origins of Nazi Germany.

(d) *Intention:* According to our definition of aggression, the child's alleged acts of aggression must reflect the intention to inflict pain or damage.

(e) *Involvement:* Does the extent to which children feel personally involved in watching the actions of cartoon mice correspond to what we assume happens during the learning of aggressiveness in everyday life (to which our theory refers)? The degree of involvement would seem to be an important aspect of research not only into aggression but also into keeping the peace. Perhaps it ought to be taken into consideration when classifying aggressive acts. Thus the assumed delivery of electric shocks, by way of a switching device, to persons one cannot observe, might in certain respects be representative of the pressing of the atomic button. For here, too, those responsible do not soil their hands with blood or their minds with unspeakable guilt. It would also be highly interesting to classify weapons, including verbal ones, by the extent to which those using them are aware of the damage they cause. The button-pushers would probably refuse to throttle or stab any one of the countless children who die as a result of their button-pressing activities. Now, it is often extremely difficult to involve our experimental subjects very deeply in the experimental set-up we present to them. Thus if we deliberately disappoint or annoy them in order to test the F-A hypothesis, we usually do so in an artificial situation, with the result that most of the subjects, generally volunteers, do not take the whole thing very seriously. Hence the leader of the experiment must devise increasingly laborious deception techniques. The publication of such ruses (e.g. Milgram's experiment (1966) in popular journals, only serves to make the experimental subjects even more suspicious. A detailed analysis of the chances of deceiving experimental subjects can be found in Stricker *et al.* (1969).

Some authors naïvely ignore the question of whether or not their experiments are representative. Thus when Elmadjian (see Chapter 4) argued that field players are more aggressive than goalkeepers, he based this conclusion on the analysis of their respective catecholamine levels, but failed to establish any links between the function of field players and their alleged aggressiveness.

## 4. Intensity measurements

The problem of measuring intensities is particularly acute in psychology. We shall therefore consider it at some length.

### MEASURING AGGRESSION

If, for instance, we wish to determine whether or not the intensity of aggression changes with age, we must be able to compare a host of aggressive acts with one another. To make such comparisons we can use numbers, i.e. try to 'measure' the respective degrees of intensity. According to Campbell (1938; quoted in Sixtle 1967), measurement is the 'correlation of numbers with objects in such a way that certain relations between numbers reflect similar relations between objects'.

In our case, the 'objects' are aggressive acts. In theory, they can be correlated in various ways, e.g. by the damage they cause. Thus we can compare aggressive acts two at a time and try to determine which has caused greater damage, and how much. The type of relation we employ is that of 'greater/smaller'. Any set of aggressive acts together with the relations defined for this set constitutes an 'empirical relational system' (see Suppes and Zinnes 1963).

The construction of an empirical relational system for the case of aggression raises the following problems:

1. Our criteria must be clearly defined. We would, for example, have to explain what type of injury we intend to measure, i.e. whether we propose to confine ourselves to physical injuries or whether we also consider other types. We must also agree on the method of determining which of two injuries is the greater.
2. Our criteria must allow of reliable conclusions; in our example, everyone should be agreed which of two injuries is the greater.
3. One and the same criterion does not have to be applicable to all types of aggression. If it applies to material damage, for instance, then it would be particularly suited to the case of physical aggression but hardly to that of verbal aggression.

The search for a reliable means of measuring all forms of aggression is exceedingly arduous. If we wish to compare only two types of aggression, defined by distinct criteria, we are forced to search for a criterion set over both. The latter is provided, for instance, by classical test theory (cf. Fischer 1968). Just as this algorithm helps us to make a quantitative comparison between the respective intensities of two qualitatively distinct faculties, e.g. intelligence and neurotic behaviour, by determinations of the deviation of either from their respective mean values (at a given distribution), so we can also compare the intensities of two distinct forms of aggression. Before we do so, we must first construct an intensity scale for each, and this is true of the comparison of any number of aggressive acts. A simple scale of this type might take the form of a numerical series. Here every aggressive act is assigned a number, in such a way that the relations between the numbers reflect the relations between the intensities of the aggressive acts. Thus the third most violent act of aggression may be assigned the number '3'. In principle, before we can measure aggression, we must be able to specify the empirical and numerical relations and the rules governing them, and also whether they are homomorphic, i.e. whether the same number can always be assigned to the same aggressive act.

Such expressions as 'measuring aggression' may be responsible for the misconception that aggression as such is the variable we are measuring. But just as 'measuring men' means determining their length, weight, intelligence, etc., so also 'measuring aggression' means trying to determine the strength of the intention to cause damage, etc. And in the same way as we can make an almost unlimited number of 'human measurements', so we can define a vast number of 'aggression measurements'. Whether or not we have chosen the correct standard of measurement is a problem in representation. We thus see once again, though from a different viewpoint, that operational definitions do not bear on aggression as such – no more, for instance, than the operational definition of human height defines the whole man. Levin and Wardwell (1962) have listed a large number of measurements applicable to aggression. In order to make these measurements as objective as possible, many workers in the field have designed experimental and instrumental arrangements including the one in which the subject believes that he is delivering electric shocks of greater or lesser intensity to others (cf. Buss 1961, p. 47). The 'Bobo-doll' which registers the intensity of the punches it receives (Bandura and Walters 1964) has also attracted wide attention. However, the exemplary objectivity of these techniques is no guarantee that they provide an accurate measure of aggression. Thus one of the adult subjects may have realized that the delivery of shocks is purely fictitious, or one of the children might have given the doll a hard but playful blow.

## MEASURING AGGRESSIVENESS

When we measure aggressiveness, we are trying to compare individuals.

If aggressiveness is indeed the psychological predisposition to commit acts of aggression, then such comparisons are best based on the performance of acts of aggression, or at least on the subjects' attitude to fictitious acts of aggression. The acts themselves can be classified and measured in the way described in the preceding section, so that it becomes possible to compare the relative aggressiveness of two persons. The resulting evaluations and the persons involved may be said to constitute an empirical relational system of the second order. The latter, plus the corresponding numerical relational system and the function that maps the former homomorphically on to a subsystem of the latter, make up an aggressiveness scale (cf. Suppes and Zinnes 1963). Here we cannot enter into the relationship between the empirical relation of the first order (which comprises acts of aggression) and the empirical relation of the second order (which includes persons) and shall simply look at several problems posed by current methods of measuring aggressiveness (i.e. of methods that do not treat explicitly of the relationships between the two empirical relational systems).

Psychologists often construct tests involving a series of problems, the solution of which is meant to throw statistical light on the intensity of individual dispositions. In the case of aggressiveness, they might study the literature, consult their colleagues, and then compile a list of appropriate items (e.g. 'I confess that I sometimes enjoy hurting others' – Item 6 in the F-aggression questionnaire, cf. Selg 1968, p. 166). Next

166

they have the questionnaire completed by a fairly large number of individuals (e.g. a group of middle-school pupils). Then the items are analysed statistically and some, i.e. those that do not satisfy the rules of the test model, are rejected. The subjects are generally tested more than once so as to ensure that all the items retained satisfy the demands of the test model – or until the psychologists lose patience, for such procedures are laborious and costly. If the psychologists do not make certain that every item is sufficiently representative of the theoretical concept of aggressiveness they are employing, and if they fail to find out how the statistical elimination of certain items affects the particular concept of aggressiveness they have adopted, then they cannot tell what the test is measuring. (For a critical account of item selection, see Loevinger 1957; Holzkamp 1964.) This is true even if the results of the test enable them to make fairly accurate predictions of, say, the frequency of aggressive acts committed by certain persons. Similarly, if they know that an intelligence test helps to predict professional success, and if the same prediction can also be made by reference to social status, they are not entitled to conclude that social status is a measure of intelligence. The designer of an aggressiveness test may object that the items themselves make it clear that what they are measuring is aggressiveness, but this he is only entitled to do if he has first tested whether his items are representative, or else he might equally well have chosen other items. It is the choice of items which dictates what type of aggressiveness is being measured. So far no particular choice has been able to establish itself as 'the' measure of aggressiveness. Hence it is much better to speak of different kinds of aggressiveness.

If an aggressiveness test contains items about asocial behaviour (the item we have described might be an example), care should be taken to allow for deliberate attempts to create a good impression.[4] Such allowances have already been built into various questionnaires (e.g. into the Minnesota Multiphasic Personality Inventory, cf. Hathaway *et al.* 1951). Other response styles that tend to falsify the results of the test can also be taken into account (cf. Berg 1967).

The usefulness of quantifiable psychological data is now granted by most people. Those who wish to compare human actions reliably (and that means controllably) must be able to measure these actions by precisely definable standards. This concern with measurement imposes certain restrictions on the use of psychological concepts (such as aggressiveness), and if these restrictions are ignored, measurement may degenerate into pseudo-measurement.

## 5. Theoretical concepts and experiences gained from their application in research and everyday life

Our conception of aggression is an invention, not a discovery. The question of what aggression and aggressiveness are 'in reality' cannot be answered. What matters is whether our conception proves useful (in the sense we have explained) in research and everyday life. To ensure that it does, it must be kept under constant scrutiny and changed whenever the need arises. Important during any particular state of research is the distinction between empirical assertions about aggression (or aggressiveness) which become increasingly precise, and the prevailing theoretical conception (including the definitions). Without an overriding theory all interpretations must remain arbitrary; conversely, the theory must be changed if experiments prove that it is false. In other words, theory and practice are closely interrelated. If we change the theory, then we must make corresponding changes to all statements based upon it. And with every such change, we necessarily change the special object of a particular research project.

168

## 6. Need for, and limitations of, empirical studies of aggression

Valid theories about certain sectors of the world must lend themselves to empirical verification in that sector. Now, empirical research into aggression is restricted by the following factors (to mention only a few):

1. The investigator must confine himself to certain (idealized) aspects of aggression. Now while this reservation applies to research in all the sciences, physics included, it is particularly marked in psychology, where a relatively large number of variables must be drastically reduced for the sake of experimental rigour.
2. Severe moral limits are set to the experimental study of human aggression.
3. The results of aggression research only apply under certain conditions (cf. Bandura and Walters 1963, p. 114; Merz 1965, p. 588). They partly reflect the prevailing cultural and social climate (cf. Holzkamp 1970). Thus research in a state that is anxious to imbue its citizens with a hatred of certain ethnic groups may well arrive at quite different conclusions from research undertaken in a state that is anxious to foster the idea of neighbourly love.

## 7. Final comment

We have tried to look at several aspects of the conceptual delimitation and application of such psychological concepts as 'aggression' and 'aggressiveness'. In so doing we have dwelt at some length on methodological problems, because the choice of method has a decisive influence on the object of analysis. Though we have kept deliberately to empirical research, no one can deny that 'aggression' raises a host of social questions that empirical psychology cannot answer

169

unaided. One such question might be: ought we to do something about aggression, and if so, what? The marked lack of collaboration between 'experimental' and 'social' scientists is due largely to a lack of consensus on the role of the social sciences. Even empirical psychology, advanced though its methods undoubtedly are, is only beginning to look like a 'normal science' (Kuhn 1967). By 'normal science' Kuhn refers to the general body of problems, methods, theories and habits of a science that is no longer torn by factional or methodological conflicts. So long as aggression research remains 'abnormal' in this sense, it must remain bogged down in arguments about fundamentals, no matter how many fresh details it may bring to light (cf. Kaufmann 1966; or Feshbach 1969). However, the fact that a universally accepted theory of aggression is unlikely to emerge in the foreseeable future does not entitle anyone to ignore the results obtained so far, particularly not if he is concerned to ensure that human beings inflict less suffering on one another than they have done in the past.

### Notes

1. Psychologists are not agreed on the meaning of 'objectivity' (cf. Bass and Berg, 1959); they generally label a state of affairs 'objective' if a number of independent observers agree on it between themselves.
2. For a critique of physicalism in psychology, cf. Smedlund (1955); Holzkamp (1964).
3. Founded by the physicist Bridgeman in 1927. For his importance to psychology, see, particularly, Stevens (1939); Patt (1945); Skinner (1945); Ellis (1956); Holzkamp (1964).
4. cf. Edwards (1957).

170

# EDITOR'S POSTSCRIPT

# EDITOR'S POSTSCRIPT

The authors of this book have not tried to conceal the fact that they, as psychologists, are attacking the popular and influential doctrines of Freud,[1] Lorenz and their followers, men whose fame rests more on literary originality than on scientific objectivity. They challenge psychoanalysts, above all, to devote the next few decades to research and, for the rest, to hold their counsel. Familiar old hypotheses such as the Oedipus and castration complexes, the death instinct, and so on, recur in psychoanalytical texts time and again, thanks to an 'incestuous' inbreeding process which operates without the benefit of empirical research. But the adoption of empirical methods is a prerequisite in this field of study, the more so as the orthodox psychoanalytical approach may be used to 'prove' everything and nothing.

This is why psychoanalysis is on the wane, and why, in the treatment of mental disorders, more recent methods (cf. Tausch 1968; Blöschl 1969) are making severe inroads into what used to be its privileged province. As a simple, but allegedly comprehensive, theoretical edifice, too, psychoanalysis is increasingly losing in credibility.

173

The socialist student movement might seem to suggest the contrary. However, the current links between psychoanalysis and socialism must be considered a passing misalliance. Freud far too readily penned phrases that must make the socialist wince, e.g. 'It is important that the morbid condition of the patient should not be allowed to blind one in making an estimate of his whole personality; those patients who do not possess a reasonable degree of education and a fairly reliable character should be refused' (1905a). Now who, at the time, enjoyed a 'reasonable degree of education'? Not the masses, who were expected to know their place. (The sham reconciliation between psychoanalysis and Marxism was criticized at length by Ludwig Marcuse in 1956.)

Those who agree with psychoanalysis in postulating an aggressive instinct are, deliberately or otherwise, fostering the continued existence of a society based uniquely on competition. For that competition is a close relative of aggression has been demonstrated by a host of 'longitudinal' analyses and experimental studies (cf. Kagan and Moss 1962; Nelson *et al.* 1969).

We must stop treating aggression as an instinct and hence as something given once and for all (cf. Chapter 3). It is bad enough that our society offers us aggressive models wherever we look, and that major acts of successful aggression can now be watched from the comfort of one's armchair. Moreover, as the theory of learning shows, even critical reports of violent acts serve as reinforcers, not as deterrents. Though we do not believe that the mass media bear sole responsibility for the growing crime rate, neither do we think that the two have no closer links than exist between, say, the consumption of oranges and road accidents.

In carrying extensive reports of horrible crimes, the mass media are not so much meeting an old need as creating a new one. By making us familiar with a host of vicious acts, they blunt our sensibilities and sense of compassion (cf. Maccoby 1968). No one can tell whether the factual reporting of acts of

174

violence produces (even rudimentary) aversion against the repetition of such acts; but it seems far more likely that it causes anxiety and hence may prove to be as undesirable as direct incitement to aggression (see pages 30-34). It is really true that a detective story only thrills its readers when it depicts the most improbable brawls and killings down to every last detail?

In the United States, no doubt under the influence of the wave of political murders (including those of President Kennedy, Martin Luther King and Robert Kennedy), there have been some early attempts to 'de-criminalize' the screen. For all that, U.S. television programmes probably continue to be the most violent of those in any country. The resulting dangers are further increased by the many aggressive models inherent in American history (lynchings, gangsters, the Wild West, the Ku-Klux-Klan – not to mention war, with which other nations are also only too familiar). Moreover, access to weapons is relatively free in the United States, so that nearly everyone can, if he likes, try out for himself whatever acts of violence he has seen on the screen. Though there are no reliable estimates of the incidence of imitative crime, it is already quite obvious that increases in certain crimes follow world-wide reports of successful actions. (We need only recall the hijackings of aeroplanes, which, according to *Der Spiegel*, No. 38, 1970, increased from thirty-two in 1968 to eighty-seven in 1969; or the many political kidnappings, bank raids and taking of hostages – as, for instance, during the 'siege' of Sidney in the summer of 1968 – which have occurred in recent times.)

The mass media should be asked to refrain from giving detailed accounts of acts of violence in their entertainment programmes and news transmissions. If they cannot or will not do so voluntarily, then society must apply the necessary controls. Unpopular though censorship undoubtedly is, it may prove the only way out from an increasingly dangerous situation – not, of course, by focusing attention on the

175

uncovered female breast, but by putting a stop to a more or less blatant glorification of violence.

No less dangerous than the display of aggressive films and the matter-of-fact reporting of gruesome details (e.g. such 'incidental' comments as: 'During this encounter, fourteen Vietcong were reported to have been killed') is the lack of positive models. An imaginative cinema or television director might try to compensate viewers for, say, the fact that fathers are rarely at home and hence have little chance to supply their children with positive models, or for the fact that many children lacking parental support grow up without any understanding of the sex-specific roles they will be expected to play in our society, with dire consequences in adolescence or adulthood (we need only think of the proportion of fatherless children among male criminals; cf. Hellmer 1966). Socially positive models are as effective as aggressive ones; not only acts of violence are imitated, but also refusals to obey aggressive orders (cf. Milgram 1966).

The present book does not contend that aggression can be stamped out altogether, or that all forms of aggression are 'bad' – it simply expresses the hope that the current trend may be significantly reduced. Even wars are not inevitable, as Klineberg has shown so impressively. Some wits claim that his description of Eskimos and others as peaceable people is false, since aggression is not unknown among them, and then go on to conclude, quite illegitimately, that the mutual recriminations of incensed Eskimos are comparable with modern warfare.

By its results, aggression research has, in fact, turned out to be peace research. The instinct hypothesis, which owes much of its popularity to Freud, and which, as a self-fulfilling prophecy,[2] probably helps to prepare the way for wars, has proved to be very tenuous. We have seen that certain nations do not engage in large-scale aggression and do not like the soldier's trade. On the other hand, we have learned how children can be taught to resort systematically to aggressive behaviour. While a great deal of further research is still needed, we are already in a position to press forward with our work of education for peace.

While man seems to be neither good nor bad, he does seem to learn aggressive behaviour early in life, long before any alternatives are to hand. As we pointed out on page 18, a fifteen-month-old can deal with many situations aggressively, but not yet constructively. Hence there is good reason for assuming that aggressive behaviour patterns are learned in advance of all others and so more thoroughly.

For the sake of completeness, we must also mention the theory that man learns to treat aggression as a privileged type of behaviour because it produces speedy and relatively conspicuous changes. Learning theory has shown that neutral environmental changes may act as reinforcers, above all those we have initiated ourselves and which therefore persuade us that we wield great 'power' over our environment. Thus children are fascinated by objects in which they can produce audible, visible or other tangible changes through simple manipulations. They will play with a typewriter for hours, even though no one praises the product of their labours.

All this can be subsumed under the principle of learning through success. It states that success need not be equated with concrete advantage, but that it can also be reflected in very modest environmental changes.

Despite the efforts of its five authors, this book is far from exhaustive. In particular, it contains no detailed account of criminality, war, the genetic factors at work in certain forms of aggressiveness, the diagnosis of aggression, institutional aggression, etc. Perhaps the authors will deal with all or some of these subjects in a later work. Their main concern has been to suggest to the layman that there are better explanatory models of aggression than those provided by the frustration-aggression hypothesis or the instinct model, so that there is no justification for blaming aggressiveness on one's own

177

instincts or on those of others. This may not be very flattering, but it is nevertheless the only logical conclusion to be drawn from the best explanatory model of the origins of aggression available at the moment: the model based on learning theory.

### Notes

1. We are here referring specifically to Freud's concept of a death instinct; for the rest we consider Freud to have been a 'great enlightener'.
2. If we believe in the irrational we are helping to make it come true. Some people are said to die on the day predicted by clairvoyants or witch doctors.

# POSTSCRIPT TO THE SECOND (GERMAN) EDITION

This book is written in an aggressive tone, which may seem odd in view of what it has to say about aggressive models.

The authors have deliberately chosen provocation, because they could think of no better way of changing the common view of aggression, moulded as it has been by psychoanalysts and ethologists. Both groups have consistently turned a deaf ear to less caustic writers. Of course, it is conceivable that they may have overlooked one or two books on the subject (indeed, it would be difficult to read *every* book on aggression), but no modern author dealing with aggression has any excuse for ignoring the contributions of Bandura and Walters, of Berkowitz or of Buss. And since this is exactly what most of them have done, year after year, we have decided to strike a more strident note.

We have made no changes to the first edition. If a third edition should be called for, some modification will be unavoidable, since important new studies have been appearing in rapid succession. Nor have we remained so many voices crying in the wilderness in Germany alone: A. Schmidt-

179

Mummendey and H. D. Schmidt, among others, have written a most illuminating book on aggressive behaviour, and the mass media, too, are beginning to heed the appeals of the opponents of violence. It would therefore seem as if the changes we have advocated are gradually finding a response from both psychologists and the public.

# BIBLIOGRAPHY

*Abzianidze, E. V.*, 1969. Vyrabotka uslovnych motivatsionnoe-motsionalnych reaktsil na baze elektricheskogo razdrazheniya gipotalamusa. (Elaboration of conditioned motivational-emotional reactions on the basis of hypothalamic electrical stimulation.) Sak artvelos SSR, Metsnierebata Akademiis Moambe, 53 (1), 197-200.

*Allen, E. K., B. M. Hart, J. S. Buell, F. R. Harris and M. M. Wolf,* 1964. Effects of social reinforcement on the isolate behaviour of a nursery school child. Child Developm., 35, 511-18.

*Allikmets, L., J. M. Delgado and R. Richards,* 1968. Intramesen-cephalic injection of imipramine, promazine and chlorprothix-ene in awake monkeys. Int. Journal of Neuropharmacology, 7, 185-93.

*Allport, G. W.,* 1937. Personality. New York.

*Allyon, T., and N. H. Azrin,* 1968. Reinforcer sampling: a technique for increasing the behaviour of mental patients. JABA 1, 13-20.

*Amsel, A.,* 1958. The role of frustrative nonreward in non-continuous reward situations. Psychol. Bull., 55, 102-19.

*Andrews, J. S., and R. C. Leaf,* 1969. Effect of amygdaloid nore-phinephrine on active-passive avoidance conflict. Proceedings of the 77th Annual Convention of the APA, 4, 899-900.

*Antons, K.,* 1970. Zur Frage des Abbaus der Persönlichkeit bei chronischem Alkoholabusus. Unveröff. Diss. Univ. Freiburg.

*Aronson, E.,* 1969. The theory of cognitive dissonance: a current perspective. In Berkowitz, L. (ed.): Advances in experimental social psychology, Vol. 4, New York.

*Aronson, E., and J. M. Carlsmith,* 1963. Effect of severity of threat on the devaluation of forbidden behaviour, J. abn. soc. Ps., 1, 66, 584-8.

*Ax, A. F.,* 1953. The physiological differentation between fear and anger in humans. Psychosom. Med., 15, 433-42.

*Axline, V.,* 1947. Play therapy. New York.

*Azrin, N. H., D. F. Hake and R. R. Hutchinson,* 1965. Elicitation of aggression by a physical blow. J. exp. anal. behav., 8, 55-7.

*Azrin, N. H., R. R. Hutchinson and D. F. Hake,* 1966. Extinction-induced aggression. J. exp. anal. behav., 9, 191-204.

*Azrin, N. H., H. B. Rubin and R. R. Hutchinson,* 1968. Biting attack by rats in response to aversive shock. J. exp. anal. behav., 11, 633-9.

*Bach, G. R.,* 1945. Young children's play fantasies. Psych. Monogr., 59, No. 2.

*Baer, D. M., and F. R. Harris,* 1963. Control of nursery school children's behaviour by programming social reinforcement from their teachers. Americ. Psychologist, 18, 343.

*Baker, J. W., and K. W. Schaie,* 1969. Effects of aggressing 'alone' or 'with another' on physiological and psychological arousal. J. Pers. Soc. Psychol., 12, 80-86.

*Bandura, A.,* 1961. Psychotherapy as a learning process. Psychol. Bull., 58, 143-59.

*Bandura, A.,* 1962. Social learning through imitation. In Jones, M. R. (ed.): Nebraska symposium on motivation. Lincoln.

*Bandura, A.,* 1965. Vicarious processes: a case of no-trial learning. In Berkowitz, L. (ed.): Advances in experimental social psychology, Vol. 2. New York.

*Bandura, A.,* 1968. Social-learning theory of identificatory processes. In Goslin, D. A. and D. C. Glass (eds.): Handbook of socialization theory and research. Chicago.

*Bandura, A., and A. C. Huston,* 1961. Identification as a process of incidental learning. J. abn. soc. Psychol., 63, 311-18.

*Bandura, A., D. Ross and S. A. Ross,* 1963. Imitation of film-mediated aggressive models. J. abn. soc. Psychol., 66, 3-11.

*Bandura, A., D. Ross and S. A. Ross,* 1964. Vicarious reinforcement and imitative learning. In Staats, A. W. (ed.): Human learning. New York.

*Bandura, A., and R. H. Walters,* 1959. Adolescent aggression. New York.

*Bandura, A., and R. H. Walters,* 1963. Aggression. In Stevenson, H. W. (ed.): Child Psychology. 62. NSSE Chicago.

*Bandura, A., and R. H. Walters,* 1964. Social Learning and Personality Development. New York.

*Bard, P.,* 1928. A diencephalic mechanism for the expression of rage with special reference to the sympathetic nervous system. Amer. J. Physiol., 84, 480-515.

*Bard, P., and V. B. Mountcastle,* 1947. Some forebrain mechanisms involved in expression of rage with special reference to suppression of angry behavior. Proc. Assn. Res. Nerv. Ment. Disease, 27, 362-404.

Barendregt, J. T., and F. S. Van Dam, 1969. Experimentelle Neurosen durch Beherrschung von Emotionen (Begleittext zum Film). Amsterdam.

Barker, R., T. Dembo and K. Lewin, 1941. Frustration and regression: an experiment with young children. Univ. of Iowa Studies. Studies in Child Welfare, 18, No. 1.

Barnett, S. A., 1968. On the hazards of analogies. In A. F. M. Montagu (ed.): Man and aggression. New York.

Baron, R. A., 1970. Attraction toward the model and model's competence as determinants of adult imitative behavior. J. pers. soc. Psychol., 14, 345-51.

Baron, R. A., and C. R. Kepner, 1970. Model's behavior and attraction toward the model as determinants of adult aggressive behavior. J. person. soc. Psychol., 1970, 14, 335-44.

Barrett, Beatrice H., 1962. Reduction of rate of multiple tics by free operant conditioning methods. J. nerv. ment. disease, 135, 187-95.

Barrish, H. H., M. Saunders and M. M. Wolf, 1969. Good behavior game: effects of individual contingencies for group consequences on disruptive behavior in a classroom. JABA 2, 119-24.

Bass, B. M., and I. A. Berg (eds.), 1959. Objective approaches to Personality Assessment. Princeton, New York.

Bateson, G., 1941. The frustration-aggression-hypothesis and culture. Psychol. Rev., 48, 350-55.

Becker, W. C., C. H. Madsen, C. R. Arnold and D. R. Thomas, 1967. The contingent use of teacher attention and praise in reducing classroom behavior problems. J. spec. Educ., 1, 287-307.

Belschner, W., 1968. Ein empirischer Beitrag zur Konstruktion des Foto-Hand-Tests, Unveröff. Diss. Univ. Freiburg.

Belschner, W., and D. Hoffman (in prep.). Untersuchung über den Zusammenhang von Lehrerverhalten und soziometrischem Status von Schülern.

Belschner, W., G. Lischke and H. Selg, 1971. Foto-Hand-Test (FHT) zur Erfassung der Aggressivität, Freiburg, 1971.

Belschner, W., and F. Schott (in prep.). Eine Inhaltsanalyse von Gute-Nacht-Geschichten dreier westdeutscher Rundfunkanstalten.

Berg, J. A., 1967. Response set in personality assessment, Chicago.

Bergius, R., 1960. Behavioristische Konzeptionen zur Persönlichkeitstheorie. In: Handbuch der Psychologie, Vol. 4. Göttingen.

183

*Bergius, R.*, 1967. Friede als soziales Verhalten und Erleben. In: Vom Frieden, Niedersächs. Landeszentrale für polit. Bildung, 93-113, Hannover.

*Bergquist, E. H.*, 1970. Output pathways of hypothalamic mechanisms for sexual, aggressive, and other motivated behaviors in opossum. J. of Comp. Physiological Psychol., 1970, 70, 389-98.

*Berkowitz, L.*, 1958. The expression and reduction of hostility. Psychol. Bull., 1958, 55, 257-83.

*Berkowitz, L.*, 1962. Aggression: A Social Psychological Analysis, New York/Toronto/London/San Francisco.

*Berkowitz, L., and R. G. Geen*, 1966. Film violence and the cue properties of available targets. J. pers. soc. psychol., 3, 525-30.

*Berkowitz, L., and D. A. Knurek*, 1969. Label-mediated hostility generalization. J. pers. soc. psychol., 13, 200-6.

*Berkowitz, L., J. B. Lepinski and E. J. Angulo*, 1969. Awareness of own anger level and subsequent aggression. J. Pers. Soc. Psychol., 11, 3, 293-300.

*Berkowitz, L., and E. R. Rawlings*, 1963. Effects of film violence on imitation against subsequent aggression. J. abnorm. soc. Psychol., 66, 405-12.

*Biermann, G.*, 1969. Kindeszüchtigung und Kindesmisshandlung. Munich.

*Bindra, D.*, 1959. Motivation, a systematic reinterpretation. New York.

*Blöschl, L.*, 1969. Behohnung und Bestrafung im Lernexperiment. Weinheim.

*Blöschl, L.*, 1969. Grundlagen und Methoden der Verhaltenstherapie. Berne/Stuttgart/Vienna.

*Boehlke, K. W., and B. E. Eleftherion*, 1967. Levels of monoamine oxidase in the brain of C S 7 B 1/6 J mice after exposure to defeat. Nature, 213, 5077, 739-40.

*Bostow, D. E., and J. B. Bailey*, 1969. Modification of severe disruptive and aggressive behavior using brief timeout and reinforcement procedures. JABA, 31-7.

*Bridgeman, P. W.*, 1927. The logic of modern physics. New York.

*Broden, M., C. Bruce, M. A. Mitchell, V. Carter and R. V. Hall*, (in proof). Effects of teacher attention on study behaviour of two boys at adjacent desks.

*Brown, G. D., and V. O. Tyler*, 1968. Time-out from reinforcement: a technique for dethroning the "duke" of an institutionalized delinquent group. J. Child Psychol. Psychiatry Allied Disc., 9, 203-11.

BIBLIOGRAPHY

*Brown, J. S.,* 1961. The motivation of behavior. New York/ Toronto/London.

*Brown, J. S., and J. E. Farber,* 1951. Emotions conceptualized as intervening variables – with suggestion toward a theory of frustration. Psychol. Bull., 48, 465-95.

*Brown, P., and R. Elliott,* 1965. Control of aggression in a nursery school class. J. exp. Child Psychol., 2, 103-7.

*Bruner, J., and L. Postman,* 1956. An approach to social perception. In Dennis, W. (ed.): Current trends in social psychology. Pittsburgh.

*Buehler, R. E., C. R. Patterson and J. M. Furniss,* 1966. The reinforcement of behavior in institutional settings. Beh. Res. Ther., 4, 157-67.

*Bunnell, B. N.,* 1966. Amygdaloid lesions and social dominance in the hooded rat. Psychonomic science, 6, 93-4.

*Bunnell, B. N., and M. H. Smith,* 1966. Septal lesions and aggressiveness in the cotton rat. Psychonomic Science, 6, 443-4.

*Burchard, J., and V. O. Tyler,* 1965. The modification of delinquent behavior through operant conditioning. Beh. Res. Ther., 2, 245-50.

*Burgess, M. M., R. S. Reivicl and J. J. Suverman,* 1968. Effects of frustration and aggression on physiological arousal level in depressed subjects. Perc. Motor Skills, 27, 743-9.

*Buss, A. H.,* 1961. The psychology of aggression. New York/ London.

*Buss, A. H.,* 1963. Physical aggression in relation to different frustrations. J. abn. soc. Psychol, 67, 1-7.

*Buss, A. H.,* 1966. Instrumentality of aggression, feedback, and frustration as determinants of physical aggression. J. pers. soc. Psychol., 3, 153-62.


*Candland, D. K., et al.,* 1970. Squirrel monkey heart rate during formation of status orders. J. Comp. Physiolog. Psychol., 70, 417-23.

*Cannon, W. B.,* 1929. Bodily changes in pain, hunger, fear and rage. New York.

*Cappell, H., and B. Latané,* 1969. Effects of alcohol and caffeine on the social and emotional behaviour of the rat. Quarterly Journal of Studies in Alcohol, 30, 345-56.

*Carlson, C. S., C. R. Arnold, W. C. Becker and C. H. Madsen,* 1968. The elimination of tantrum behavior of a child in an elementary classroom. Behav. Res. Ther., 6, 117-19.

*Carpenter, L., Jr*, 1957. Relations of aggressions in the personality to outcome with electroconvulsive shock therapy. J. gen. Psychol., 57, 3-22.

*Chapman, W. P., et al.*, 1954. Physiological evidence concerning the importance of amygdaloid nuclear region in the integration of articulatory function and emotion in man. Science, 120, 949-50.

*Chittenden, G. E.*, 1942. An experimental study in measuring and modifying assertive behavior in young children. Monogr. soc. res. child develpm., 7, No. 1.

*Clausewitz, C.*, 1832. Vom Kriege, Bonn.

*Cowan, P. A., and R. H. Walters*, 1963. Studies of reinforcement of aggression. I. Effects of scheduling. Child Developm., 34, 543-51.

*Cronbach, L. J., and P. E. Meehl*, 1955. Construct validity in psychological tests. Psychol. Bull., 52, 281-302.

*Dann, H.-D.*, 1967. Genetische Aspekte aggressiven Verhaltens. Z. ersieh.-wiss. For., 1, 3-37.

*Dann, H.-D.*, 1970. Auswirkungen des Gewährens versus Unterbindung aggressiven Verhaltens auf kognitive Prozesse. Schw. Z. Psych. Anw., 29, 257-72.

*Davitz, J. R.*, 1952. The effects of previous training on postfrustration behavior. J. abn. soc. Ps., 47, 309-15.

*Delgado, J. M. R.*, 1963. Cerebral heterostimulation in a monkey colony. Science, 241, 161-3.

*Delgado, J. M. R., and L. M. Kitahata*, 1967. Reversible depression of hippocampus by local injections of anaesthetics in monkeys. Electroencephalography and clinical Neurophysiology, 22, 453-64.

*Detjen, E. W., and M. F. Detjen*, 1963. Elementary school guidance. New York.

*Dodsen, J. T.*, 1917. Relative value of reward and punishment in habit formation. Psychobiology, 1, 231-76.

*Dollard, J., L. W. Doob, N. E. Miller, O. H. Mowrer and R. R. Sears*, 1939. Frustration and aggression. New Haven.

*Dorsch, F.*, 1959. Psychologisches Wörterbuch, Hamburg/Berne.

*Drath, E.-M.*, 1969. Über den Einfluss von Frustration auf Handtest-Ergebnisse bei Kindern. Unveröff. Diplomarbeit., Freiburg.

*Edwards, A. L.*, 1957. The social desirability variable in personality research. New York.

186

*Edwards, D. A.*, 1969. Early androgen stimulation and aggressive behavior in male and female mice. Physiology and Behavior, 4 (3), 333-8.

*Egger, M. D., and J. P. Flynn*, 1963. Effects of electrical stimulation of the amygdalae on hypothalamically elicited attack behavior in cats. J. neurophysiol., 26, 705-20.

*Eleftheriou, B. E., and K. W. Boehlke*, 1967. Brain monoamine oxidase in mice after exposure to aggression and defeat. Science, 155, 3770, 1963-4.

*Eleftheriou, B. E., and R. L. Church*, 1968. Brain 5-hydroxy-tryptophan decarboxylase in mice after exposure to aggression and defeat. Physiology and Behaviour, 3, 2, 323-5.

*Eleftheriou, B. E., et al.*, 1963. Effect of repeated exposure to aggression and defeat on plasma and pituitary levels of thyreotropin. Physiology and Behavior, 3, 3, 467-9.

*Ellis, A.*, 1956. An operational reformulation of some of the basic principles of psychoanalysis. In Feigle, H., and M. Scriven (eds.): Minnesota Studies in the Philosophy of Science, Vol. I. Minneapolis.

*Ellison, G. D., and J. B. Flynn*, 1968. Organized aggressive behavior in cats after surgical isolation of the hypothalamus. Archives Italiennes de Biology, 106, 1-20.

*Epstein, R.*, 1966. Aggression toward outgroups as a function of authoritarianism and imitation of aggressive models. J. Pers. soc. Psychol., 3, 574-9.

*Eron, L. D.*, 1963. Relationships of TV viewing habits and aggressive behavior in children. J. abn. soc. Psychol., 67, 193-6.

*Eron, L. D., L. O. Walder, R. Toigo, and M. M. Lefkowitz*, 1963. Social class, parental punishment for aggression, and child aggression. Child develom., 34, 849-67.

*Eyferth, K.*, 1964. Das Lernen von Haltungen, Bedürfnissen und sozialen Verhaltensweisen. In Bergius, R. (ed.): Hanbduch der Psychologie, Vol. I, 2. Göttingen.

*Eysenck, H. J., et al.*, 1972. Encyclopaedia of Psychology. London.

*Ferster, C. B.*, 1958. Reinforcement and punishment in the control of human behavior by social agencies. Psychiat. res. reports, 10, 101-18.

*Ferster, C. B., and J. B. Appel*, 1961. Punishment of S△ responding in match to sample by timeout from positive reinforcement. J. exp. anal. beh., 4, 45-56.

*Feshbach, S.*, 1955. The drive-reducing function of fantasy behavior. J. abn. soc. psychol., 50, 3-11.

*Feshbach*, *S.*, 1956. The catharsis hypothesis and some consequences of interaction with aggressive and neutral play objects. J. pers., 24, 449-62.

*Feshbach*, *S.*, 1961. The stimulating versus cathartic effect of a vicarious aggressive activity. J. abn. soc. psychol., 63, 381-5.

*Feshbach*, *S.*, 1964. The function of aggression and the regulation of aggressive drive. Psychol. Rev., 257-72.

*Finch*, *D. M.*, *and R. S. Surwil*, 1968. The effects of amygdalectomy on shock-induced fighting behaviour in rats. Psychonomic Science, 10, 360-70.

*Fine*, *B. J.*, *and D. R. Sweeney*, 1967. Socio-economic background, aggression and catecholamine excretion. Psych. Reports, 20, 11-18.

*Fine*, *B. J.*, *and D. R. Sweeney*, 1968. Personality traits, and situational factors, and catecholamine excretion. J. Exp. Res. Person., 3, 15-27.

*Fischer*, *G. H.* (ed.), 1968. Psychologische Testtheorie. Berne/ Stuttgart.

*Fishman*, *C. G.*, 1965. Need for approval and the expression of aggression under varying conditions of frustration. J. pers. soc. Psychol., 2, 809-16.

*Flynn*, *J. B.*, 1967. The neural basis of aggression in cats. In Glass, D. C.: Neuropsychology and emotion. New York.

*Foppa*, *K.*, 1966. Lernen, Gedächtnis, Verhalten. Cologne.

*Freedmann*, *J. L.*, 1965. Long-term behavioral effects of cognitive dissonance. J. exp. soc. Ps., 1, 145-55.

*Freud*, *S.*, 1904. Über Psychotherapie. Ges. W., Vol. V, 1904. (On Psychotherapy, Collected Papers I, Institute of Psychoanalysis and Hogarth Press, London, 1924.)

*Freud*, *S.*, 1905. Drei Abhandlungen zur Sexualtheorie. Ges. W., Vol. V. (Three Contributions to the Theory of Sex, Nervous and Mental Disease Publishing Company, New York and Washington, 1910.)

*Freud*, *S.*, 1909. Analyse der Phobie eines fünfjährigen Knaben. Ges. W., Vol. VII. (Analysis of a Phobia in a Five-year-old Boy, Collected Papers III.)

*Freud*, *S.*, 1915a. Triebe und Triebschicksale. Ges. W., Vol. X. (Instincts and their Vicissitudes, Collected Papers IV.)

*Freud*, *S.*, 1915b. Zeitgemässes über Krieg und Tod. Ges. W., Vol. X. (Thoughts for the Times on War and Death, Collected Papers IV.)

*Freud*, *S.*, 1917. Vorlesungen zur Einführung in die Psychoanalyse.

Ges. W., Vol. XI. (Introductory Lectures to Psychoanalysis, Boni and Liveright, New York, 1920.)

*Freud, S.*, 1922. Jenseits des Lustprinzips. Ges. W., Vol. XIII. (Beyond the Pleasure Principle, International Psychoanalytic Press, London, 1922.)

*Freud, S.*, 1923. Das Ich und das Es. Ges. W., Vol. XIII. (The Ego and the Id, Institute of Psychoanalysis and Hogarth Press, London, 1927.)

*Freud, S.*, 1924. Das ökonomische Problem des Masochismus. Ges. W., Vol. XIII. (The Economic Problem in Masochism, Collected Papers II.)

*Freud, S.*, 1925. Die Verneinung. Ges. W., Vol. XIV. (On Negation, International Journal of Psychoanalysis, VI, 1923.)

*Freud, S.*, 1930. Das Unbehagen in der Kultur. Ges. W., Vol. XIV. (Civilization and its Discontents, Institute of Psychoanalysis and Hogarth Press, London, 1946.)

*Freud, S.*, 1933a. Neue Folge der Vorlesungen zur Einführung in die Psychoanalyse. Ges. W., Vol. XV. (New Introductory Lectures on Psychoanalysis, Garden City Publications Company, New York, 1933.)

*Freud, S.*, 1933 b. Warum Krieg? Ges. W., Vol. XVI. (Why War? Standard Edition, Vol. XXII, Institute of Psychoanalysis and Hogarth Press, London, 1932-6.)

*Freud, S.*, 1938. Abriss der Psychoanlyse. Ges. W., Vol. XVII. (An Outline of Psychoanalysis, International Journal of Psychoanalysis, XXI, 1940.)

*Fuller, J. L., and W. R. Thompson*, 1960. Behavior Genetics. New York.

*Funkenstein, D., S. H. King, M. Drolette*, 1954. The direction of anger during a laboratory stress-induction situation. Psychosom. Med., 16, 404-13.

*Galef, B. G., Jr*, 1970. Aggression and timidity: Responses to novelty in feral Norway rats. J. Compar. Physiol. Psychol., 70, 370-81.

*Gambaro, S., and A. J. Rabin*, 1969. Diastolic blood pressure responses following direct and displaced aggression after anger arousal in high- and low-guilt subjects. J. pers. soc. Psychol., 12, 87-94.

*Geen, R. G., and E. C. O'Neal*, 1969. Activation of cue-elicited aggression by general arousal. J. pers. soc. Psychol., 11, 289-92.

*Glueck, S., and E. Glueck*, 1950. Unraveling juvenile delinquency. New York.

*Goddard, G. V.*, 1964. Function of the amygdalae. Psychol. Bull., 62, 89-109.

*Graumann, C. F.*, 1956. Social Perception. Die Motivation der Wahrnehmung in neueren amerikansichen Untersuchungen. Z. exp. angew. Psychol., 3, 605-61.

*Graumann, C. F.*, 1960. Eigenschaften als Problem der Persönlichkeitsforschung. In Lersch, Ph. and H. Thomae (eds.): Handbuch der Psychologie, Vol. IV, Göttingen.

*Guthrie, E. R.*, 1952. The psychology of learning. New York.

*Hall, C. S.*, 1951. The genetics of behavior. In Stevens, S. S. (ed.): Handbook of experimental psychology. New York.

*Hall, V. R., et al.*, 1968. Instructing beginning teachers in reinforcement procedures which improve classroom control. JABA, 1, 315-22.

*Haner, C. F., and P. A. Brown*, 1955. Clarification of the instigation to action concept in the frustration-aggression hypothesis. J. abn. soc. Psychol., 51, 204-6.

*Harlow, H. F., and M. K. Harlow*, 1961. A study of animal affection. Nat. Hist., 70, 48-55.

*Hartmann, D. P.*, 1969. Influence of symbolically modeled instrumental aggression and pain cues on aggressive behavior. J. pers. soc. Psychol., 11, 280-88.

*Hartmann, H., E. Kris and R. Loewenstein*, 1949. Notes on the theory of aggression. In: The psychoanalytic study of the child. III/IV, 9-36.

*Hartrup, W. W., and Y. Himeno*, 1959. Social isolation versus interaction with adults in relation to aggression in preschool children. J. abn. soc. Psychol., 59, 17-22.

*Haseloff, O. W., and E. Jorswieck*, 1970. Psychologie des Lernens. Berlin.

*Hathaway, S. R., and J. C. McKinley*, 1951. Minnesota Multiphasic Personality Inventory, New York.

*Hävernick, W.*, 1964. "Schläge" als Strafe – ein Bestandteil der Familiensitte in volkskundlicher Sicht. Hamburg.

*Hawkins, R. P., et al.*, 1966. Behavior therapy in the home: amelioration of problem parent-child relations with the patient in therapeutic role. J. exp. child Psychol., 4, 99-107.

*Heath, R. G., R. R. Monroe and W. A. Mechle*, 1955. Stimulation of the amygdaloid nucleus in a schizophrenic patient. Amer. J. Psychiat., 11, 862-3.

*Hebb, D. O.*, 1949. The organization of behavior. New York.

*Hellmer, J.*, 1966. Jugendkriminalität in unserer Zeit. Frankfurt-am-Main.

*Herrmann, T.*, 1969. Lehrbuch der empirischen Persönlichkeits-forschung. Göttingen.

*Hess, W. R.*, 1954. Das Zwischenhirn. Basle.

*Hess, W. R.*, 1956. Hypothalamus und Thalamus. Stuttgart.

*Hicks, D. J.*, 1965. Imitation and retention of film-mediated aggressive peer and adult models. J. Pers. soc. Psychol., 2, 97-100.

*Hicks, D. J.*, 1968. Effects in co-observer's sanctions and adult presence on imitative aggression. Child Develpm., 39, 303-9.

*Hill, W. F.*, 1960. Learning theory and the acquisition of values. Psychol. Rev., 67, 317-31.

*Hörmann, H.*, 1964. Aussagemöglichkeiten psychologischer Diagnostik. Göttingen.

*Hofstätter, P. R.*, 1957. Gruppendynamik. Hamburg.

*Hofstätter, P. R.*, 1957. Psychologie. Frankfurt.

*Hokanson, J. E.*, 1961. The effects of frustration and anxiety on overt aggression. J. abnorm. soc. Psychol., 62, 346-51.

*Hokanson, J. E., and M. Burgess*, 1962. The effects of status, type of frustration, and aggression on vascular processes. J. abn. soc. Psychol., 65, 232-7.

*Hokanson, J. E., and M. Burgess*, 1962. The effects of three types of aggression in vascular processes. J. abn. soc. Psychol., 64, 446-9.

*Hokanson, J. E., M. Burgess and M. F. Cohen*, 1963. Effect of displaced aggression on systolic blood pressure. J. abn. soc. Psychol., 67, 214-18.

*Hokanson, J. E. and S. Shetler*, 1961. The effect of overt aggression on psychological arousal level. J. abn. soc. Psychol., 1961, 63, 446-8.

*Hokanson, J. E., K. R. Willers and E. Koropsak*, 1968. The modification of autonomic responses during aggressive interchange. J. person., 36, 386-404.

*Holmes, D. S.*, 1966. Effects of overt aggression on level of physiological arousal. J. pers. soc. Psychol., 4, 189-94.

*Holst, E. v. and U. v. Saint Paul*, 1960. Vom Wirkungsgefüge der Triebe. Naturwiss., 1960, 47, 409-22.

*Holst, E. v. and U. v. Saint Paul*, 1962. Electrically controlled behavior. Scient. Amer., 206, 50-59.

*Holzkamp, K.*, 1964. Theorie und Experiment in der Psychologie. Berlin.

*Holzkamp, K.*, 1968. Wissenschaft als Handlung. Versuch einer neuen Grundlegung der Wissenschaftslehre. Berlin.

*Holzkamp, K.*, 1969. Reinforcement durch Blickkontakt: eine empirische Studie. Z. exp. angew. Psychol., 16, 538-60.

*Holzkamp, K.*, 1970. Zum Problem der Relevanz psychologischer Forschung für die Praxis. Psychol. Rundschau, 21, 1-22.

*Horn, K.*, 1967. Dressur oder Erziehung – Schlagrituale und ihre gesellschaftliche Funktion. Frankfurt.

*Hovland, C. J.*, 1954. Effects in the mass-media of communication. In Lindzey, G. (ed.): Handbook of Social Psychology, Vol. II. Cambridge.

*Hull, C. L.*, 1943. Principles of behavior. New York.

*Hull, C. L.*, 1952. A behavior system. New Haven.

*Ilfeld, F. W.*, 1969. Overview of the causes and prevention of violence. Archives of gen. Psychiatry, 20, 675-89.

*Jackson, L.*, 1954. Aggression and its interpretation. London.

*James, W. H., and B. J. Rotter*, 1958. Partial and 100 percent reinforcement under chance and skill conditions. J. exp. Psychol., 55, 397-403.

*Johnstone, M. K., et al.*, 1966. An application of reinforcement principles to development of motor skills in a young child. Child Developm., 37, 379-87.

*Jones, E.*, 1953-7. Sigmund Freud: Life and Work, Vols. I-III. London, Hogarth Press.

*Kagan, J., and H. A. Moss*, 1962. Birth to maturity. New York/ London.

*Kahn, M.*, 1966. The physiology of catharsis. J. pers. soc. Psychol., 3, 278-86.

*Kahn, M. W., and W. E. Kirk*, 1968. The concept of aggression: A review and reformulation. Psychol. Rec. 18, 559-73.

*Kaiser, K.*, 1970. Das Drohsystem überwinden. In: Der Spiegel, No. 20, 220-25. Hamburg.

*Kamlah, W., and P. Lorenzen*, 1967. Logische Propädeutik oder Vorschule des vernünftigen Redens. Mannheim.

*Karli, P.*, 1958. Hormones steroides et comportement d'aggression interspécifique rat-souris. J. Physiol. Path. Gen., 50, 346-7.

*Karli, P., and M. Vergnes*, 1963. Rôle du rhinéncephale dans le contrôle du comportement d'aggression interspécifique rat-souris. Journal de Physiologie, 55, 272-3.

*Kaufmann, H.*, 1965. Definitions and Methodology in the Study of Aggression. Psychol. Bull., 64, 351-64.

*Kenny, D. T.*, 1953. An experimental test of the catharsis theory of aggression. Ann Arbor.

*Kermani, E. J.*, 1969. "Aggression." Biophysical aspects. Diseases of the Nervous System, 30, 407-14.

*Klineberg, O.*, 1966. Die menschliche Dimension in den internationalen Beziehungen. Berne/Stuttgart.

*Klopper, A.*, 1964. Physiological background to aggression. In Carthy, J. D., and F. J. Elbing: The natural history of aggression. London.

*Kornadt, H.-J.*, 1966. Einflüsse der Erziehung auf die Aggressivitätsgenese. In Herrmann, Th. (ed.): Psychologie der Erziehungsstile. Göttingen.

*Kraft, V.*, 1950. Der Wiener Kreis. Der Ursprung des Neopositivismus. Vienna.

*Kregarman, J. J., and P. Worchel*, 1961. Arbitrariness of frustration and aggression. J. abn. soc. Psychol., 63, 183-7.

*Kuhn, T. S.*, 1967. Die Struktur wissenschaftlicher Revolution. Frankfurt-am-Main.

*Kuiper, P. C.*, 1964. Aggression und das metapsychologische Modell. Paper read to the Frankf. Psychoanalyt. Congress.

*Langelüddecke, A.*, 1959. Gerichtliche Psychiatrie. Berlin.

*Larder, D. L.*, 1962. Effect of aggressive story content on non-verbal play behavior. Psychol. Rep., 11, 14.

*Latané, B., and A. J. Arrowood*, 1963, Emotional arousal and task performance. J. appl. Psychol., 47, 234-327.

*Laties, V. G.*, 1961. Modification of affect, social behavior and performance by sleep deprivation and drugs. J. Psychiat. Res., 1, 12-24.

*Lawrence, D. H., and L. Festinger*, 1962. Determinants and re-inforcements: the psychology of insufficient rewards. Stanford.

*Lawson, R.*, 1965. Frustration. New York/London.

*Lefkowitz, M., et al.*, 1955. Status factors in pedestrian violation of traffic signals. J. abn. soc. Psychol., 51, 704-6.

*Leonhardt, R. L.*, 1967. Auf der Sexwelle. In Die Zeit, 1 Dec. 1967. Hamburg.

*Levin, H., amd V. Turgeon*, 1957. The influence of mother's presence on children's doll play aggression. J. abn. soc. Ps., 55, 304-8.

*Levin, M., and E. Wardwell*, 1962. The research uses of doll play. Psychol Bull., 59, 27-56.

*Levinson, P. K., and J. P. Flynn*, 1965. The objects attacked by cats during stimulation of the hypothalamus. Animal Behavior, 13, 217-20.

*Levy, L. H.*, 1963. Psychological interpretation. New York/London.

*Leyhausen, P.*, 1960. Verhaltensstudien an Katzen. Berlin.

*Little, K. B., and D. K. Adams*, 1965. The catharsis value of aggression fantasy. J. proj. Techn., 29, 336-40.

*Loevinger, J.*, 1957. Objective tests as instruments of psychological theory. Psychol. Rep., Monogr. Suppl. 9.

*Lorenz, K.*, 1937. Über die Bildung des Instinktbegriffes. Die Naturwissensch. 25, No. 19.

*Lorenz, K.*, 1966. On Aggression. London.

*Lovaas, I. O.*, 1961a. Interaction between verbal and nonverbal behavior. Child developm., 32, 329-36.

*Lovaas, I. O.*, 1961b. Effect of exposure to symbolic aggression on aggressive behavior. Child developm., 32, 37-44.

*Loy, D. L., and J. W. Turnbull*, 1964. Indirect assessment of anger disposition. J. proj. techn. person. ass., 28, 314-21.

*Maccoby, E. E.*, 1954. Why do children watch television? Publ. Opin. Quart., 18, 239-44.

*Madsen, C. H., W. C. Becker, D. R. Thomas, L. Koser and E. Plager*, 1968. An analysis of the reinforcing function of 'sit down' commands. In Parker, R. K. (ed.): Readings in educational psychology. Boston.

*Madsen, C. H., W. C. Becker and D. R. Thomas*, 1968. Rules, praise and ignoring: elements of elementary classroom control. J. appl. behav. anal., 1, 139-50.

*Magoun, H. W.*, 1958. The waking brain. Springfield, Ill.

*Maier, N. R. F.*, 1949. Frustration. New York.

*Mallik, S. K., and B. R. McCandless*, 1966. A study of catharsis of aggression. J. pers. soc. Psychol., 4, 591-6.

*Marcuse, L.*, 1965. Sigmund Freud. Hamburg.

*McCord, J., and W. McCord*, 1958. The effects of parental role models on criminality. J. soc. Issues, 14, 66-74.

*McDonnell, M. F., and J. B. Flynn*, 1964. Attack elicited by stimulation of the thalamus in cats. Science, 44, 1249-50.

*McDonnell, M. F., and J. B. Flynn*, 1966. Sensory control of hypothalamic attack. Animal Behavior, 13, 399-405.

*McDougall, W.*, 1947. Outline of Psychology, London.

*McKenzie, H. S., M. Clark, M. M. Wolf, R. Kothera and C. Benson*, 1968. Behavior modification of children with learning disabilities using grades as tokens and allowances as back up reinforcers. Except. Children, 34, 745-52.

*Meichenbaum, D. M., K. S. Bowers and R. R. Ross*, 1968. Modification of classroom behavior of institutionalized female adolescent offenders. Behav. res. ther. 6, 343-53.

*Menke-Glückert, P.*, 1969. Friedensstrategien. Hamburg.

*Menninger, W. C.*, 1948. Recreation and mental health. Recreation, 42, 340-46.

*Merz, F.*, 1965. Aggression und Aggressionstrieb. In Thomae, H. (ed.): Handbuch der Psychologie, Vol. II. Göttingen.

*Milgram, S.*, 1966. Einige Bedingungen von Autoritätsgehorsam und seiner Verweigerung. Z. exp. angew. Psychol., 13, 433-63.

*Miller, N. E.*, 1941. The frustration-aggression hypothesis. Psychol. Rev., 48, 337-42.

*Miller, N. E.*, 1948. Studies of fear as an acquirable drive. J. exp. Psychol., 38, 89-101.

*Miller, N. E.*, 1960. Learning resistance to pain and fear: effects of overlearning, exposure and rewarded exposure in content. J. exp. Psychol., 60, 137-45.

*Miller, N. E., and J. Dollard*, 1941. Social learning and imitation. New Haven.

*Mischel, W., and J. Grusec*, 1966. Determinants of the rehearsal and transmission of neutral and aversive behaviors. J. pers. soc. Psychol., 3, 197-205.

*Mitscherlich, A.* (ed.), 1969a. Bis hierher und nicht weiter – Ist die menschliche Aggression unbefriedbar? Munich.

*Mitscherlich, A.*, 1969b. Aggression ist eine Grundmacht des Lebens – Rede zur Verleihung des Friedenspreises des deutschen Buchhandels, 12 October 1969. In Der Spiegel, No. 42, 206-12, Hamburg.

*Mitscherlich, A.*, 1969c. Die Idee des Friedens und die menschliche Aggressivität. Frankfurt.

*Montagu, M. F. A.* (ed.), 1968. Man and aggression. New York.

*Morden, B., et al.*, 1968. Effects of rapid eye movement (REM) sleep deprivation on shock-induced fighting. Psychology and Behavior, 3, 425-32.

*Mowrer, O. H.*, 1960. Learning theory and behavior. New York.

*Moyer, K. E.*, 1969. Internal impulses to aggression. Transactions of the New York Academy of Sciences, 31, 109-14.

*Müller, H. A.*, 1960. Anfangsschwierigkeiten des Volksschullehrers. Die deutsche Schule, 52, 348-61.

*Mussen, P. H., and E. Rutherford*, 1961. Effects of aggressive cartoons on children's aggressive play. abn. J. soc. Psychol., 62, 461-4.

*Nelson, J. D., D. M. Gelfand and D. P. Hartmann*, 1969. Children's aggression following competition and exposure to an aggressive model. Child development, 40, 1085-97.

*Nestle, W.*, 1938. Der Friedensgedanke in der antiken Welt. Leipzig.

*Newcomb, T. M.*, 1966. Social Psychology. London.

*Niedersächsische Landeszentrale für Politische Bildung*, 1967. Vom Frieden. Hannover.

*Nighswander, J. K., and G. R. Mayer*, 1969. Catharsis: a means of elementary school student's aggressive behaviors? Pers. Guidance J., 47, 461-6.

*Nowak, D. W., and M. J. Lerner*, 1960. The effect of preparatory actions on beliefs concerning nuclear war: a test of some alternative explanations. J. soc. Ps., 70, 11-121.

*Oerter, R.*, 1967. Moderne Entwicklungspsychologie. Donauwörth.

*Olds, J.*, 1969. Self-Stimulation of the Brain. In Gross, C. G., and H. P. Zeigler: Readings in psychiological Psychology: Motivation. New York.

*Orlans, H.*, 1963. Infant care and personality. In Rachman, S. (ed.): Critical essays on psychoanalysis. London.

*Palmer, S.*, 1960. Frustration, aggression and murder. J. abn. soc. Psychol., 60, 430-32.

*Panksepp, J., and J. Trowill*, 1969. Electrically induced affective attack from the hypothalamus of the albino rat. Psychonomic Science, 16, 118-9.

*Pastore, N.*, 1952. The role of arbitrariness in the frustration-aggression hypothesis. J. abn. soc. Psychol., 47, 728-31.

*Patterson, G., R. Littman and W. Bricker*, 1967. Assertive behavior in children. Monogr. of the Society for Research in Child Developm., 32, 1-43.

*Pawlow, I. P.*, 1953. Zwanzigjährige Erfahrungen mit dem objectiven Studium der Höheren Nerventätigkeit. Sämtl. Werke, Vol. 3, Berlin.

*Plack, A.*, 1967. Die Gesellschaft und das Böse. Munich.

*Pratt, C. C.*, 1945. Operationism in psychology. In Boring, E. G. (ed.): Symposium on operationism. Psychol. Rev., 52, 262-9.

*Pribram, K. H.*, 1967. Emotion: Steps toward a neuropsychological theory. In Glass, D. C. (ed.): Neuropsychology and emotion. New York.

*Rachman, S.*, 1965. Pain-elicited aggression and behavior therapy. Psychol. Rec., 15, 465.

*Rattner, J.*, 1970. Aggression und menschliche Natur. Olten/ Freiburg.

*Raumer, K. V.*, 1953. Ewiger Friede – Friedensrufe und Friedenspläne seit der Renaissance, Freiburg.

*Reeves, A. G., and F. Plum*, 1969. Hyperphagia, rage, and dementia accompanying a ventromedial hypothalamic neoplasm. Archives of Neurology, 20, 616-24.

*Rein, H., and M. Schneider*, 1960. Einführung in die Physiologie des Menschen. Berlin.

*Roberts, W. W., and H. O. Kiess*, 1964. Motivational properties of hypothalamic aggression in cats. J. compar. physiol. Psychol., 58, 187-93.

*Rosekrans, M. A., and W. W. Hartrup*, 1967. Imitative influences of consistent and inconsistent response consequences to a model on aggressive behavior in children. J. pers. soc. Psychol., 7, 429-34.

*Rosenbaum, M. E., and R. Decharms*, 1960. Direct and vicarious reduction of hostility. J. abn. soc. Psychol., 60, 105-11.

*Rosenzweig, S.*, 1934. Types of reaction to frustration: a heuristic classification. J. abn. soc. Psychol., 29, 298-300.

*Rosvold, H. E., A. F. Mirsky and K. H. Pribram*, 1954. Influence of amygdalectomy on social behavior in monkeys. J. Comp. Physiol. Psychol., 47, 173-8.

*Roth, E. L.*, 1963. Über die Begriffsbildung in der Persönlichkeitspsychologie. Jb. Psychol., Psychotherapie und Med. Anthrop., 10, 139-48.

*Roth, E. L.*, 1969. Persönlichkeitspsychologie. Stuttgart/Berlin/ Cologne/ Mainz, 1969.

*Russell, B.*, 1957. Why I am Not a Christian. London.

*Schachter, J.*, 1957. Pain, fear, and anger in hypertensives and normotensives. Psychosom. Med., 19, 17:29.

*Schachter, J., and B. Latané*, 1964. Crime, cognition and the automatic nervous system. In *D. Levine* (ed.), 1962: Nebraska symposium on motivation. Lincoln.

*Schachter, J., and J. E. Singer*, 1962. Cognitive, social, and physiological determinants of emotional state. Psychol. Rev., 69, 379-99.

197

*Schachter, J., and L. Wheeler*, 1962. Epinephrine, chlorpromazine, and amusement. J. abnorm. soc. Psychol., 65, 121-8.

*Schneewind, K. A.*, 1969. Methodisches Denken in der Psychologie. Berne/Stuttgart/Vienna.

*Schönbach, P.*, 1967. James Bond – Anreiz zur Aggression? In Merz, F. (ed.): Bericht 25. Kg. DGP, 1966. Göttingen.

*Schreiner, L., and A. Kling*, 1956. Rhinencephalon and behavior. Amer. J. Physiol., 184, 486-90.

*Schwitzgebel, R.*, 1964. Short-term operant conditioning of adolescent offenders on socially relevant variables. Thesis, Brandeis Univ.

*Schwitzgebel, R.*, 1969. Preliminary socialization for psychotherapy of behavior disordered adolescents. J. cons. clinic. Psychol., 33, 71-7.

*Schwitzgebel, R., and D. A. Kolb*, 1964. Inducing behavior change in adolescent delinquents. Behav. res. ther., 1, 297-304.

*Scott, J. P.*, 1958. Aggression. Chicago.

*Scott, P. M., R. V. Burton and M. R. Yarrow*, 1967. Social reinforcement under natural conditions. Child developm., 38, 53-63.

*Sears, R. R.*, 1941. Nonaggressive reactions to frustration. Psychol. Rev., 48, 343-6.

*Sears, R. R., E. E. Maccoby and H. Levin*, 1957. Patterns of child rearing. Evanston.

*Sears, R. R., J. W. Whiting, V. Nowlis and P. S. Sears*, 1953. Some child-rearing antecedents of aggression and dependency in young children. Genet. psychol. monogr. 47, 135-234.

*Secord, P. E., and C. W. Backman*, 1964. Social Psychology. New York.

*Seiffert, H.*, 1969. Einführung in die Wissenschaftstheorie 1. Munich.

*Selg, H.*, 1966. Einführung in die experimentelle Psychologie. Stuttgart.

*Selg, H.*, 1968. Diagnostik der Aggressivität. Göttingen.

*Selg, H.*, 1972. Entwicklung und Lernen. Braunschweig.

*Selinger, H. E., and G. Bermant*, 1967. Hormonal control of aggressive behavior in Japanese quail. Behavior, 28, 255-68.

*Selye, H.*, 1956. The stress of life. New York.

*Sixtl, F.*, 1967. Messmethoden der Psychologie. Weinheim.

*Silverman, I., and D. Kleinman*, 1967. A response deviance interpretation of the effects of experimentally induced frustration on prejudice. J. exp. res. pers., 2, 150-53.

*Skinner, B. F.*, 1945. The operational analysis of psychological terms. Psychol. Rev., 52, 270-77.

*Skinner, B. F.*, 1938. The behavior of organisms. New York.

*Sloane, H. N., M. K. Johnston and S. W. Bijou*, 1967. Successive modification of aggressive behavior and aggressive fantasy play by management of contingencies. J. Child. Ps. and Psychiatry and allied Disciplines, 8, 217-26.

*Soares, L. M., and A. T. Soares*, 1969. Social learning and social violence. Proceedings of the 77th Annual Convention of the APA, 4, 463-4.

*Solomon, R. L., J. K. Kamin and L. C. Wynne*, 1953. Traumatic avoidance learning: the outcomes of several extinction procedures with dogs. J. abn. soc. Psychol., 48, 291-302.

*Smedslund, J.*, 1955. The epistemological foundations of behaviorism. A critique. Acta Psychologica, 11, 412-31.

*Smith, D. E., M. B. King and B. G. Habel*, 1969. Killing: Cholinergic control in the lateral hypothalamus. Proceedings of the 77th Annual Convention of the APA, 4, 895-6.

*Sprague, J. M., W. W. Chambers and E. Stellar*, 1961. Attentive, affective and adaptive behavior in the Cat. Science, 133, 165-73.

*Staats, A. W., J. R. Finley, K. A. Minke and M. Wolf*, 1964. Reinforcement variables in the control of unit reading responses. J. exp. anal. behav., 7, 139-49.

*Stevens, S. S.*, 1939. Psychology and the science of science. Psychol. Bull., 36, 221-63.

*Stewart, O. C.*, 1968. Lorenz/Margulin on the Ute. In M. F. A. Montagu (ed.): Man and aggression. New York.

*Stiller, M.*, 1970. Gewalt – die einzige Lösung. Südd. Zeitung, 9 April.

*Stokman, C. L., and M. Glusman*, 1968. A procedure to quantify hypothalamically elicited agonistic behavior in the cat. Psychonomic Science, 11, 325-6.

*Straus, E.*, 1956. Vom Sinn der Sinne. Berlin-Heidelberg.

*Stricker, L. J., S. Messick and D. N. Jackson*, 1969. Evaluation deception in psychological research. Psychol. Bull., 71, 343-51.

*Summers, T. B., and W. W. Kalber*, 1962. Amygdalectomy: Effects in cats and a survey of its present status. Amer. J. Physiol., 203, 1117-19.

*Suppes, P., and J. L. Zinnes*, 1963. Basic measurement theory. In Luce, R. D., R. Bush and E. Galanter (eds.): Handbook of mathematical psychology, Vol. I. New York.

*Tack, W. H.*, 1970. Messung als Repräsentation empirischer Gegebenheiten. Z. exp. angew. Psychol., 17, 184-212.

*Tausch, A., R. Tausch and B. Fittkau*, 1967. Merkmalszusammenhänge der verbalen Interaktion und kritische Überprüfung typologischer Verhaltensknozepte. Z. exp. angew. Ps., 14, 522-41.

*Tausch, R.*, 1968. Gesprächspsychotherapie. Göttingen.

*Taylor, S. P.*, 1967. Aggressive behavior and physiological arousal as a function of provocation and the tendency to inhibit aggression. J. Pers. 35, 297-310.

*Taylor, S. P., and S. Epstein*, 1967. Aggression as a function of the interaction of the sex of the aggressor and the sex of the victim. J. pers., 35, 474-85.

*Terris, W., and M. Barnes*, 1969. Learned resistance to punishment and subsequent responsiveness to the same and novel punishments. Psychon. Sc., 15, 49-50.

*Terris, W., and D. K. Rahhal*, 1969. Generalized resistance to the effects of psychological stressors. J. pers. soc. Psychol., 13, 93-7.

*Terris, W., and D. K. Rahhal*, 1969. Learning to resist mild or intense shock punishment and subsequent resistance to airblast punishment. Psychon. Sc., 15, 45-6.

*Terris, W., and S. Wechkin*, 1967. Learning to resist the effects of punishment. Psychon. Sc. 7, 169-70.

*Textor, R.*, 1968. A cross-cultural summary. New Haven.

*Thelen, M. H., and W. Soltz*, 1969. The effect of vicarious reinforcement on imitation in 2 social-racial groups. Child Developm., 40, 879-88.

*Thibaut, J. W., and H. W. Riecken*, 1955. Authoritarianism, status, and the communication of aggression. Hum. Relat., 8, 95-120.

*Thoman, E. V., R. L. Commer and S. Levine*, 1970. Lactation suppresses adrenal corticosteroid activity and aggressiveness in rats. J. Comp. Physiol. Psychol., 70, 364-9.

*Thomas, D. R., W. C. Becker and M. Armstrong*, 1968. Production and elimination of disruptive classroom behavior by systematically varying teachers' behavior. JABA, 1, 35-45.

*Thor, D. H.*, 1969. Chemical induction of traumatic fighting behavior. Proceedings of the 77th Annual Convention of APA, 4, 883-4.

*Thorndike, E. L.*, 1903. Educational Psychology. New York.

*Thorndike, E. L.*, 1913. The psychology of learning – Educational Psychology, Vol. II. New York.

*Tinbergen, N.*, 1956. Instinktlehre. Berlin.

*Tolman, E. C.*, 1932. Purposive behavior in animals and men. New York.

*Tolman, E. C.*, 1959. Principles of purposive behavior. In Koch, S. (ed.): Psychology: a study of a science. New York.

*Toman, W.*, 1954. Dynamik der Motive. Frankfurt-am-Main/ Vienna.

*Traxel, W.*, 1968. Über Gegenstand und Methode der Psychologie. Berne/Stuttgart.

*Tyler, V. O., and G. D. Brown*, 1967. The use of swift, brief isolation as a group control device for institutionalized delinquents. Behav. res. ther., 5, 1-9.

*Tyler, V. O., and G. D. Brown*, 1968. Token reinforcement of academic performance with institutionalized delinquent boys. J. educ. Ps., 59, 164-8.

*Ullrich, W.*, 1964. Die Kindesentführung. Neuwied.

*Ulrich, R., M. Wolfe and S. Dulaney*, 1969. Punishment of shock-induced aggression. J. exp. anal. behav., 12, 1009-15.

*Vernon, W. M.*, 1969. Animal aggression. Review of research. Genetic monographs, 80, 3-20.

*Walters, R. H.*, 1962. Enhancement of punitive behavior by audiovisual displays. Science, 872-3.

*Walters, R. H.*, 1966. Implications of laboratory studies of aggression for the control and regulation of violence. Annals of the Amerc. Acad. of Political and Social Science, 364, 60-72.

*Walters, R. H., and M. Brown*, 1963. Studies of reinforcement of aggression: III. Transfer of responses to an interpersonal situation. Child developm., 34, 563-71.

*Walters, R. H., and M. Brown*, 1964. A test of the high-magnitude theory of aggression. J. exp. child psychol., 1, 376-87.

*Walters, R. H., and L. Demkov*, 1963. Timing of punishment as a determinant of response inhibition. Child Developm., 34, 207-14.

*Walters, R. H., M. Leat and L. Mezei*, 1963. Inhibition and disinhibition of response through empathetic learning. Canad. J. Psychol., 17, 235-43.

*Ward, M. H., and B. L. Baker*, 1968. Reinforcement therapy in the classroom. J. appl. behav. anal. 1, 323-8.

*Wasman, M., and J. P. Flynn*, 1962. Directed attack elicited from the hypothalamus. Arch. Neurol., 6, 220-27.

*Watson, J. B.*, 1914. Behavior. New York.

*Watson, J. B.*, 1919. Psychology from the standpoint of a behaviorist. Philadelphia.

201

*Weber, P. G.*, 1966. Rohrstock in Schule und Heim. Stuttgart.

*Wepman, J. M., and R. W. Heine*, 1963. Concepts of personality. Chicago.

*Wetterling, H.*, 1964. Effekt: Schwachsinn. Die Zeit. No. 9.

*Wetzel, A. B., R. L. Conner and S. Levine*, 1967. Shock-induced fighting in septal-lesioned rats. Psychon. Sc., 9, 133-4.

*Whiting, J. W. M.*, 1941. Becoming a Kwoma. New Haven.

*Wieczerkowski, W., et al.*, 1969. Verminderung von Angst und Neurotizismus bei Schülern durch positive Bekräftigungen von Lehren im Schulunterricht. Z. Entw.-Ps. Päd. Ps., 1, 3-12.

*Wiener, N.*, 1961. Cybernetics, Cambridge, Mass.

*Williams, C. D.*, 1959. The elimination of tantrum behavior by extinction procedures. J. abn. soc. Psych., 59, 269.

*Wittenborn, J. R.*, 1954. The development of adoptive children. New York.

*Wittgenstein, L.*, 1967. Philosophical Investigations. Oxford.

*Wolf, E.*, 1964. Rohrstock- Erziehung. Die Zeit, 29 May.

*Wolf, M. M., T. Risley and H. Mess*, 1964. Application of operant conditioning procedures to the behavior problems of an autistic child. Behav. res. ther. 1, 305-12.

*Wood, C. D.*, 1958. Behavioral changes following discrete lesions of temporal brain structures. Neurology, 8, 215-20.

*Worchel, P.*, 1957. Catharsis and the relief of hostility. J. abnorm. soc. Psychol., 55, 238-43.

*Yasakochi, G.*, 1960. Emotional responses elicited by electrical stimulation of the Hypothalamus in cat. Folia psychiat. neurol., 14, 260-67.

*Yerkes, R. M., and J. D. Dodson*, 1908. The relation of strength of stimulus to rapidity of habit-formation. J. comp. neurol. Psychol., 18, 459-82.

*Zimmerman, E. H., and J. Zimmerman*, 1962. The alternation of behavior in a special classroom situation. J. exp. anal. behav., 5, 59-60.